MULTIETHNIC MINISTRY AND DIASPORA MISSIONS IN ACTION

A Case Study of the Wu Chang Church of Kaohsiung, Taiwan

Enoch Wan & John Kuo

Multiethnic Ministry and Diaspora Missions in Action:
A Case Study of the Wu Chang Church of Kaohsiung, Taiwan

Printed in the United States of America

First Printing: December 2019
Western Seminary Press

ISBN-13: 978-1-949201-06-2

WESTERN SEMINARY
Center for Diaspora
and Relational Research

Center for Diaspora & Relational Research
Western Seminary
5511 SE Hawthorne Blvd.
Portland, OR 97215, USA

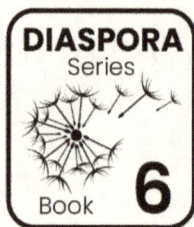

DIASPORA Series

Book **6**

CONTENTS

CHAPTER 1

INTRODUCTION

Background of the book

T he research for this book was conducted by John Kuo for his doctoral dissertation at Western Seminary under the supervision of Enoch Wan, PhD, Director, Doctor of Intercultural Studies. John Kuo has had multiethnic ministry experiences in the U.S. for more than a decade and is the first to introduce such paradigm to Taiwan. He is also the first known practitioner of multiethnic ministries to conduct a study on multiethnic ministry in a local church context in Taiwan. In terms of conducting such action research in this host church, namely the Wu Chang Church in Taiwan, John is also the best person because of his passion to promote unity in the body of Christ and his experience with diaspora missions. Occasionally, the use of "I" in the book is intended to be more personable in reference to John Kuo who collected the data for this research.

Purpose

The purpose of this book is to showcase multiethnic ministry and diaspora missions in action at the Wu Chang Church of Kaohsiung, Taiwan.

Definition of key terms

Multiethnic Church (MEC): is defined as a church with at least two ethnic groups, with at least twenty percent of the congregants from one or more ethnic backgrounds differing from the congregation as a whole. MEC is sometimes referred to as multiracial or multicultural church. There is also a multi-congregational church, which allows various language services to be conducted in the same location yet belonging to the same church body. In this book, Multiethnic Church will be used to represent this diversity.

New Residents in Taiwan: the so-called fifth ethnic group of Taiwan. New Residents is a term used by the government in Taiwan to give designation to two groups of foreigners living in Taiwan. One is foreign spouses from mainland China, Southeast Asia, and other parts of the world. Another group is contract migrant workers temporarily living in Taiwan for employment in factories, for major construction projects, and domestic household care for elderly and disabled.

Relational Theology/Missiology: proposed by Enoch Wan, relational theology is offered as a counterbalance to the functionalism-oriented theology and practices of Western missions. Relational theology seeks to draw from the relational harmony of the Triune God, emphasizing the importance of relations within the body of Christ. "Relational missiology," then, "is the practical outworking of relational theology in carrying out the *missio Dei* and fulfilling the Great Commission."

Multiculturalism: as understood in sociology and political science, multiculturalism seeks an ideal harmonious multicultural society based on humanistic and relativistic views of culture and spirituality. Its assumption is that in a multicultural and pluralistic society, respect for diversity and tolerance for differences will allow a society with various cultural/ethnic groups to co-exist.

Diaspora Missiology: the term "diaspora" is a reference to "people living outside their place of origin" and "diaspora missiology" is "a missiological framework for understanding and participating in God's redemptive mission among diaspora groups."

Diaspora Missions: according to Wan, Diaspora Missions is "practice emerging from the paradigm of 'diaspora missiology' which includes ministering to diasporic groups and ministering through/beyond to fulfill the Great Commission." There are four types of diaspora missions as listed below:

Missions *to* the Diaspora — reach the diaspora groups in forms of Evangelism or pre-evangelistic social services, then disciple them to become worshipping communities and congregations.

Missions *through* the Diaspora — diaspora Christians reaching out to their kinsmen through networks of friendship and kinship in host countries, their homelands, and abroad.

Missions *by* and *beyond* the Diaspora — motivating and mobilizing diaspora Christians for cross-cultural missions to other ethnic groups in their host countries, homelands, and abroad.

Missions *with* the Diaspora — mobilizing non-diasporic Christians individually and institutionally to partner with   diasporic groups and congregations (Wan 2014:6).

Organization of the book

In addition to "introduction" and "conclusion," there are five chapters. Thus begins the presentation of the Wu Chang Church of Kaohsiung, Taiwan in chapter 2. Foundational understandings of multiethnic ministries is covered in chapter 3. Readers will find ethnographic description and the practice of multiethnic ministries in chapter 4, diaspora missions in chapter 5, with Multiethnic Ministry and diaspora missions in action in chapter 6, from the perspective of the Wu Chang Church.

CHAPTER 2

THE WU CHANG CHURCH OF KAOHSIUNG, TAIWAN

Introduction

E ntering the 21st century the world has witnessed more people migrating across the globe more frequently than ever before. Moreover, the waves of immigration are not exclusively arriving on Western shores. Major countries in Asia, whose economic and geopolitical forces are on the rise in the global scene, are now on the receiving end of this immigration. Among the three key economies in East Asia (from data retrieved in 2012), Japan hosted a total of 2.2 million foreigners;[1] South Korea, which traditionally has been a very homogenous society, had 590,000 foreigners residing in the country;[2] and Taiwan reported a total of 990,000 foreign nationals residing among its 23 million residents. That means, in 2012, one out of 23 people in Taiwan was of foreign descent. As of June, 2012, 465,279 expatriates were living or working in Taiwan, and one out of six couples in Taiwan was an international marriage.[3] This does not include the four major ethnic groups already calling this island their home. Whether one is aware of it or not, the nations have come to Taiwan.

In December, 2016, Wu Chang Church celebrated her 40th anniversary. With nearly three thousand attendees and ten daughter churches, Wu Chang is one of several megachurches in the city of Kaohsiung, Taiwan with deep rooted purpose for missions. In this chapter we will look at Wu Chang

---

[1] *United Nations' Trends in Total Migrant Stock*: The 2008 Revision,<http://esa.un.org/migration > 01.09.12.
[2] Nathan Schwartzman, "Government Release Statistics on Foreigners in Korea," TravelWireAsia, 2011 <http://www.travelwireasia.com/2011/06/government-releases-statistics-on-foreigners-in-korea/> 01.09.12.
[3] According to National Immigration Agency, the total number of international marriages, which includes cross-strait marriages totaled 21,516 in the year 2011. See the excel page titled "Foreign Residents" dated 12.20.12.<http://www.immigration.gov.tw/lp.asp?ctNode=29986&CtUnit=16677&BaseDSD=7&mp=2> 12.20.12.

Church's development and transformation from a small street side church to a church with missionary outreach both locally and globally. In today's age of globalization, Wu Chang Church seeks to be both local and global in her missionary endeavor. We will retrace the stages through which this church transformed from an ethnic church to a multiethnic church by deliberately reaching out to diasporas in her community.

Brief History of Conservative Baptist Mission in Taiwan

Conservative Baptist Foreign Mission Society (CBFMS), now WorldVenture, came to Taiwan in 1952 after the Communists expelled foreign missionaries from the mainland of China. The first Conservative Baptist gospel center was founded in Nantou, located in the central part of Taiwan. The mission strategy then was to reach rural areas where there was the least Christian witness. Missionaries who relocated from mainland China used Mandarin, while some of the new missionaries after the early 1950s adopted Taiwanese.[4] The purpose was to reach out to the secondary cities and townships in the least evangelized regions of Taiwan. Ethnic composition of churches in these areas was and still is primarily made up of two language groups: Mandarin-speaking mainlanders who came with their leader Chang Kai-Shek after suffering defeat in the civil war, and the Taiwanese speaking Min-Nan group, whose ancestors came to the island centuries before. In general, the Mandarin-speaking one million people were more open to the gospel; the Min-Nan speaking were more entrenched in indigenous beliefs and resistant to the gospel. However, for the CB mission, usually a given church would either have two language services or interpretation in order to reach both people groups.

CB mission endeavors included 16 churches planted and gospel centers with a membership over 1100 people between 1952 and 1970.[5] In addition to church planting, CB mission started a Bible college in 1957 in the township of Xiluo for the purpose of training local CB pastors; there is a publishing house and a large camp, Bamboo Valley Bible Camp, situated in the scenic central mountainous region of Nantou. Ralph and Ruth Covell, after relocating from mainland China, came to the east coast of Taiwan to help with a Bible translation project for the Sediq people, one of the dozen indigenous tribal people groups in Taiwan.

In the mid-1960s, the mission found out, through economic development, the ratio between urban and rural population began to change dramatically, so it shifted its mission focus to major urban centers, such as Taipei, Taichung, and Kaohsiung. In the same vein, the mission also implemented a church planting initiative that encouraged churches to be self-supporting, self-sustaining, and self-propagating.[6] It was under such a push to plant urban churches that the mission came to the port city of Kaohsiung where Wu Chang Church is located. The year 2012 marked the

---

[4] CBFMS Overseas Director Ray Buker, Sr. desired that CBFMS missionaries go to unreached people groups, so it was decided that CBFMS would start its ministry in the secondary cities of south-central Taiwan. Information gathered from CBGlobal webpage. <http://www.cbglobal.org/cb-taiwan> 09. 24. 12.

[5] CBFMS 50th Anniversary Publication 1952-2002, 中華基督教浸信宣道會五十週年紀念特刊, 6.

[6] CBFMS 50th Anniversary Publication 1952-2002, 7.

60th anniversary of the Conservative Baptist (CB) mission to Taiwan, and the movement had 42 churches that are scattered in cities as well as in rural townships in Taiwan with a membership at that time of 5,000 plus believers.

History of Wu Chang Church

In 1965, missionary couple Jim and Maggie Cummings came to Kaohsiung and started a work, which later became the San-Min CB Church. CB missionary John Branner's family along with pastor Huang Ming-ji of the San Min Church began a church plant in the Wu Jiah district (south) of Kaohsiung in 1977. The church was named Wu Chang Church after the market area where it first was founded. Wu Chang (武昌) is the appellation of a place name in China where the first shot of the successful revolution to overthrow the Qing Dynasty was fired. So the name itself always gives a hint of feistiness and drive. Actually, since the church began to make its name known in the city, this is how churches have been describing Wu Chang: a church with a passion to reach out, one full of vitality.

Stages of Wu Chang Church's Growth

This church has gone through four developmental stages, according to the church's senior pastor, Rev. John Cheng.[7] In 2012, the church had moved four times in 39 years of history. At each stage different factors contributed to the growth of the church. Stage one was mainly due to strong entrepreneurial leadership of her founding pastor along with support of CB missionaries, who intentionally encouraged Wu Chang Church to plant its first daughter church, the Nanjing Church. Power encounter and healings were recognized as breakthrough movements of this church. The second stage had to do with greater emphasis on developing the spiritual depth of the congregation, as well as a gradual opening to charismatic movement. During this stage the church hosted numerous revival conferences with domestic and international speakers from various traditions and backgrounds. Among them were the Prayer Mountain of Rev. Yonggi Cho of Korea and the Agape Ministry of America. Spiritual awakening took place among the church leadership during this time. Pastoral staff and lay leadership were in agreement, seeking personal and corporate spiritual breakthrough for this church. Although the church organizational structure was not changed, the leadership was intentional in pursuing a balance between the word of God and the works of the Holy Spirit.[8] Stage three was by and large restructuring of the church's pastoral structure by utilizing the cell group church model promoted by Faith Community Baptist Church (FCBC) of Singapore. In the early 90s, FCBC sent several waves of leaders to Taiwan to coach many denominations and individual churches about the cell church ministry model, which was researched and taught by Ralph Neighbor, Jr. and his colleagues at Touch Ministries. Many churches, including Wu Chang, adopted this cell group model and trained leaders in this concept, although the original fellowship structure remained in place. This move enabled the church raise up many lay leaders and the church began to reach out to the community. In 1996 the church established a semi-autonomous ministry called the "Community

---

[7] Wu Chang Church Thirtieth Year Anniversary Book (武昌教會三十週年特刊), 24.

[8] *Wu Chang Church Thirtieth Year Anniversary Book* (武昌教會三十週年特刊), 24.

Care Association" as her social arm to reach out and meet the needs of the community around her.[9] This ministry has now developed into a self-sustaining and self-supporting ministry that offers relief and assistance, social services, and adult education to the community around the church, including several classes of new immigrant orientation. The fourth stage, which began in 2002, is distinguished by the church's focus on missions and church planting. The church leadership has set a fifteen years' goal to plant ten churches and send out ten missionaries.[10] These goals were a result of the church's efforts to be a uniting force in the city of Kaohsiung by bringing pastors from various denominations to gather for weekly prayer and fellowship. It was during this time that the church began to send out her first missionary to China, and began to enter partnership with the Back to Jerusalem Movement (BJM) in China. Right about this time, the church purchased a partially-finished structure (2003), and with the congregation's faith to believe that God's glory would be shown through this church, they turned a skeletal eye sore on the side of a major boulevard of the city into a ten story building, now the home of this vibrant church. It stands as a witness to the faithful hand of God over more than 40 years of the history of Wu Chang Church.

Vision of Wu Chang Church

The church did not formally adopt a vision statement until stage three (1995-2002) when the church underwent an organizational change to adopt the cell group structure introduced and coached by Faith Community Baptist Church (FCBC) of Singapore, which sent coaching teams every year to Taiwan to enable churches restructure their organizations and operations. From such a change, an early-stage vision was adopted which is spelled out in four words: "Unity, Equipping, Caring, and Missions."[11] A vision statement spells out the church's mission: "To build a church that seeks to fulfill the Great Commission and honors Christ in all we do." Under this vision statement, the church has been actively engaged in domestic and foreign missions, especially to Mainland China. There were numerical goals of planting 10 churches by the year 2015 and growing the church body to be a 5,000 member church.[12] The actions included the rewording of the church's vision and mission statement at the 2011 leadership retreat and follow-up meetings, as well as the solidification of church multiethnic goals: developing the existing Taiwanese congregation and Mandarin congregation, the English congregation, and Hakka fellowship.

Summary

For Christian missions, which aim at reaching the nations (Matt. 28:18-20), the same question that has been asked for churches in North America must be posed to Taiwan churches: What are they

---

[9] *Wu Chang Church Thirtieth Year Anniversary Book* (武昌教會三十週年特刊), 25.

[10] Wu Chang Church deacons' meeting minutes, October 2012. See Appendix 2.

[11] The Chinese vi000000sion statement is 合一, 裝備, 關懷, 宣教. Wu Chang Church Thirtieth Year Anniversary Book (武昌教會三十週年特刊), 25.

[12] Wu Chang Church deacons' meeting minutes dated 01.01.12. See Appendix 2.

to do about this multiethnic/multicultural reality? Or to put it in human and relational terms, What are we to do with these aliens among us?[13] Traditionally, churches have been formed along denominational, ethnic, language, and social lines.[14] The church growth movement in the 20th century emphasized the People Groups concept and promoted church planting along these lines. However, there are some deficiencies with this model. Planting churches according to people groups may have been natural in the setting of countries like India, where a history of church missions to this ancient civilization and her caste system rooted in the Hindu traditions causes churches to be formed along those above mentioned lines. Adding to the complexity of the subcontinent are her socio-economic disparities and the big gap between urban and rural developments. The rationale for "Homogeneous Unit Principle" (HUP) based on the Indian experience may have been reasonable for that context. However, in today's diverse and globalized urban communities, where ethnic groups from around the world co-existing and mixing together is a daily reality, this principle for church development needs to be reexamined for the following reasons: First, too much effort is expended on finding personnel and financial resources in order to organize these ethnic churches in the cities where real estate prices are often hard to swallow no matter how big the groups are. Second, these ethnic churches have a generational gap between first generation immigrants and second generation. If churches are organized according to languages and ethnic backgrounds, losing the second generation is almost unavoidable for ethnic minority churches. Last and most importantly, there is a distorted picture of what a church should be, especially in an ethnically diverse urban setting. Although unintended, the homogenous ethnic church model runs the risk of rendering cross-cultural missions more as projects than a way of life for churches. It is against the globalized, diasporic, and multiethnic demographic backdrop of Taiwan that I sought to conduct this action-oriented research project on Wu Chang Church, where I currently serve.

---

[13] Enoch Wan, "Research Methodology for Diaspora Missiology and Diaspora Missions," Global Missiology. Vol.4, No.4, (March, 2007).

[14] Donald McGavran presented material on this church formation basing his findings on the churches in India. He categorized them into five basic types and four secondary types. See his work, *Ethnic Reality and the Church, Lessons from India*. (Pasadena, CA: William Carey Library, 1979).

CHAPTER 3

FOUNDATIONAL

UNDERSTANDINGS OF

MULTIETHNIC MINISTRIES

Introduction

To understand the many facets of how one should engage in multiethnic ministries in this age of globalization, one needs to look at the driving force behind the secular world's approach to inclusivity and where it fails to accomplish its lofty goal. Multiculturalism is widely adopted by countries receiving immigrants, as the social and political formula for multiethnic coexistence. However, more and more countries, especially in Europe, are finding that the traditional multicultural policy is not able to function when ethnic groups within the society do not play by the rules. Alonzo Ramirez and Enoch Wan affirm this from a study of Old Testament theology on multiethnicity and multiculturality.[15] The following statement is the assumption for His church: "God's covenant people are the inter-ethnic and intercultural manifestation of God's unity in diversity."[16]

On this notion, Dan Sheffield addresses this need for a Christian multiculturalism for church. When talking about multiculturalism and the Christian community, he mentions the need for

---

[15] Alonzo Ramirez and Enoch Wan, "A Biblical Theology of Multiethnicity and Multi-Culturality, Unity in Diversity, and God's Ultimate Purpose for Humanity." *Global Missiology*, (July 2004).
<http://www.enochwan.com/english/articles/pdf/Biblical%20Theology%20of%20Multi-Culturality.pdf>
02.11.13.
[16] Ramirez and Wan, "A Biblical Theology of Multiethnicity and Multi-Culturality, Unity in Diversity, and God's Ultimate Purpose for Humanity." *Global Missiology*, (July 2004), 4.

Christians in an ethnically-diverse community to function within the basic convictions of multiculturalism that all cultures should "...submit their values to the examination, sifting, and transformation of Scripture."[17] On this subject, Michael Cromartie provides a rare observation of how evangelicals view multiculturalism with its implications in various social and political topics.[18] On the opposite side of this acceptance of diversity within a church body, is the notion of racism. John Bartkowski, a sociologist at Mississippi State University, calls this Christian version of multiculturalism "The Multicultural Evangelicalism." Bartkowski talks about the need for Christian churches to address the issue of racial reconciliation amid cultural diversity.[19] Dennis McCallum, on the other hand, reflects on how evangelical churches respond to the multiculturalism of the postmodern age. Speaking as a pastor, he reminds readers that people are social beings and that "...the Bible is much closer to postmodernism than modernism in its portrait of members of the Christian community," instead of the lopsided emphasis on individualism.[20] It is from such an understanding of a multiethnic/multicultural communality of the church as revealed in the Scriptures that I draw wisdom and guidance.

The Biblical Mandate for Multiethnic Church: From the Jerusalem Church and Beyond

In the extensive prayer Jesus offered up for the disciples the night before His glorification He prayed to the Father that all of them may be one: "May they be brought to complete unity to let the world know ...." (John 17:22-23). After His resurrection, Jesus called the disciples together and gave them the Great Commission. The scope of the task at hand is to make disciples of all nations, baptizing them and teaching them. The fruit of such a task is the Body of Christ, the Church. During the forty days before His ascension, Jesus taught the disciples about the Kingdom of God, which is beyond Israel, global in scale. He instructed the disciples to wait in Jerusalem for the promised Holy Spirit so that they would be empowered to be His witnesses "to the ends of the earth" (Acts 1:8). The arrival of the Holy Spirit at Pentecost marked the beginning of the Church. Through various tongues, the Holy Spirit demonstrated to us that the nature of church is unity in diversity. It is the antithesis of the Tower of Babel, where humanity tried to come together on their own terms with the aim to make a name for themselves (Gen. 11:4). God came down, confused their languages, and scattered them over all the earth (Gen. 11:8). It was a human effort trying to rally people together for greatness apart from their Creator God. On the day of Pentecost, it was the Creator God Who brought the nations together

---

[17] Daniel Sheffield, *The Multicultural Leader.* (Ontario: Clements Publishing, 2005), 42.

[18] Michael Cromartie, *A Public Faith, Evangelicals, and Civic Engagement.* (Maryland: Rowman & Littlefield Publishers , 2003).

[19] John P. Bartkowski, *Promise Keepers: Servants, Soldiers, and Godly Men.* (New Brunswick, NJ: Rutgers University Press, 2004).

[20] Dennis McCallum, General Editor, *The Death of Truth: Responding to Multiculturalism, the Rejection of Reason, and the New Postmodern Diversity.* (Bloomington, Minnesota: Bethany House Publishers, 1996), 2707-2715.

to make a new creation out of diversity. Through the cross, God's purpose is to create in Himself one new man out of the two, Gentiles and Jews (Eph. 2:15). This is the biblical foundation for church.

The Jerusalem Church

Although the first church in Jerusalem was predominately a Jewish congregation, her membership consisted of many believers born and raised in the Gentile world. The first organized church in history is a church made up of Jews and various subcultures from the vast Mediterranean region. Within this church there are at least sixteen languages spoken, and Jewish and Hellenistic cultures were intertwined heavily. The interesting point is, even though it was such a mixed group, the subgroups did not branch out to build their own ethnic churches. On the contrary, from the leadership to the believers, they all dealt with their struggles and continued to stay together. An incident occurred when the Grecian Jews among the disciples "complained against the Hebraic Jews because their widows were being overlooked in the daily distribution of food" (Acts 6:1). The twelve leaders did not see the differences in languages and cultures, or even their socio-economic levels, as good enough reasons to go their separate ways. On the contrary, they called the people together and asked the disciples to choose from among them seven deacons who were "full of the Spirit and wisdom" (Acts 6:3), to deal with this distribution problem. It should be noted that they did not see this as a cultural or ethnic problem; rather, they simply focused on their shared faith. The Hellenistic Jews who complained about their widows being neglected in the daily rationing of food were satisfied when seven deacons were elected from among them to take care of the issue. They pressed on to stay as a body of believers (Acts 6:1-7). The persecution of believers following the martyrdom of Stephen sent the disciples further into the Gentile world. This was the exact command of Jesus. However, it took a time of persecution to motivate the disciples to go out.

Peter's xenophobic view was corrected by the vision from God and subsequently by the conversion of the household of Cornelius. For a simple Jewish follower of Jesus of Nazareth to have this change of view was revolutionary. Luke recorded this historic incident in detail to tell future generations how this wall between Jews and Gentiles was taken down by direct intervention from God in the latter days. That Peter's unreserved obedience was approved is clear from the outpouring of the Holy Spirit among the household of Cornelius. Peter saw this occasion as the turning point for the church and the future mission of the church. Paul's dramatic conversion experience is the landmark event for the church's formal move from a Jewish religious sect to a worldwide movement. The Apostle to the Gentiles was the God-chosen vessel to bridge these two major cultures of the first century Near Eastern world, the Greeks and the Jews, forming a new community called "Christians" (Acts 11:26).

The Antioch Church

The formation of the Antioch church demonstrates God's design for a church. Similar to today's North American context, the Mediterranean world in the first century was a multicultural society. Although the dominant culture was Greek, various provinces each maintained their distinct culture and languages. The Gospel started out from a mono-cultural Jerusalem and spread to a multicultural world outside. Let us take a closer look at how the Holy Spirit led believers in building a church after God's heart.

Three Stages of Development of the Antioch Church

First Stage: Missions to the Gentile World

The Antioch church was the result of the dispersed disciples preaching the gospel to the Gentiles after the persecution of the church in Jerusalem (Acts 11:20). This handful of believers began working outside of their comfort zone, reaching out to the Greeks. This new development was under the careful eye of the Jerusalem church. To find out about this Antioch church, they sent out Barnabas to investigate the situation. Barnabas played a crucial role in this Gentile church mission. His action and report could mean death or life to this emerging ministry. Barnabas was born in Cyprus. He himself was a Hellenistic Jew who spoke both Greek and Hebrew. Because of his encouraging spirit, his friends called him Barnabas, meaning "Son of Encouragement." The Bible says that when he saw the evidence of the grace of God, he was glad and encouraged them all to remain true to the Lord with all their heart (Acts 11:23). Praise God for Barnabas! Not only that, he even set out to Tarsus to look for Paul, who was a Roman citizen, fluent in Greek and Hebrew, had the best rabbinic training, and had experienced salvation and a willingness to serve the Lord.[21]

Second Stage: Mission with the Greek

The membership that made up the Antioch church consisted of people from various backgrounds. Its leadership team was made up of two men from Africa, one from the Mediterranean, one from Asia Minor, and one from the Middle East (Acts 4:36; 9:11; 13:1).[22] They all identified with this church and worked to build up the church. The Bible specifically says that believers were called Christians first at Antioch (Acts 11:26). The reason is simple: they demonstrated such a unique fellowship that people around them could not put them in traditional categories. This new identity they shared in Christ became their trademark.[23] Their way of life and worship brought the nature of church to life. Paul in Ephesians called this the mystery revealed to him, that through the gospel the Gentiles are heirs together with Israel, members together of one body, and sharers together of the promise in Christ Jesus (Eph. 3:6).

Third Stage: Mission from the Greek

The sending of Paul and Barnabas by the Antioch church demonstrates that they not only identified with this church, they are willing to submit to the leadership of this church. They prayed and obeyed the words of the Holy Spirit, not their own. Paul's missionary journeys started from and returned to the church in Antioch. They did not elevate their individual ethnic/cultural uniqueness; rather they were devoted to the will of God for His church. Even though Barnabas was sent by the Jerusalem church to check out the Antioch church, and Paul was invited by Barnabas to assist him, they saw themselves as members of this local body of Christ.

---

[21] Mark DeYmaz and Harry Li, *Ethnic Blends: Mixing Diversity into Your Local Church*. (Grand Rapids, Michigan: Zondervan, 2010), 42.
[22] DeYmaz and Li, *Ethnic Blends*, 42.
[23] Mark DeYmaz, *Building A Healthy Multiethnic Church: Mandate, Commitments, and Practices of a Diverse Congregation*, (San Francisco, CA: Jossey-Bass Publishers, 2007, 2010), 20.

Here one sees the evolution of Jewish-Gentile relations in the New Testament from that of division to fusion. The fact that disciples were called Christians first in Antioch indicates they must have demonstrated a way of corporate and religious life that was unprecedented and unique, so much so that the people of that city could not associate them with any particular existing religious sect. The followers of Christ reached out to one another across cultural and ethnic barriers, bypassed religious taboos, and worshipped together. It was revolutionary in the eyes of the citizens of Antioch; hence they gave this group of people a new label, "Christians." Unity does not mean uniformity. The members of the church in Antioch still retained their cultural identities, and they strived to stay and work together. Such a unity begins with a new Lord Who is above cultures and ethnicities, and held up by a mission originating from the Holy Spirit. This particular church became the biblical model for the church with a mission, and now even better understood as the church with a call to unity. Unity serves, then, both as the foundation for their mission and the end goal for the same.

Even though not all biblical records demonstrate Scriptural authority,[24] the biblical precedents quoted above clearly are prescriptive in and of themselves, for they are both the direct prayer and command of the Lord (Acts 1:8), and the actions following in obedience to the command and the leading of the Holy Spirit. It is thus Scriptural, and requires one's allegiance in action and practice. In fact, throughout history, the mission God has been directing His missionary people to bring is the message of the Kingdom exactly as it was prescribed for us in the Bible, to all peoples of the world. Churches are therefore the embodiment of this new creation. They are not simply a group of believers. Rather they are brothers and sisters of the same Heavenly Father. This should be what church is like: In today's multiethnic urban settings, we have a clear biblical mandate to reach out to others and bring all ethnic groups represented in the community together. And if churches are like that, we will once again make the name "Christians" both meaningful and telling. This is the heart of the Father, the prayer of our Lord, and the heart of the Holy Spirit. Let the church continue to practice the Lord's commission and commandment in and through His church until the end of the world (Matt. 28:19). In summary, the church in Antioch is a good model for developing multiethnic church. It is both achievable and biblical for today's western churches, and, as a result of people movements associated with globalization, for more rapidly developing multiethnic contexts of the world like that of Taiwan. Churches today can and must look back to biblical teachings and records to come up with a Scriptural principle for their development in today's multicultural society where God has placed them. In a word, the local churches must respond to, and reflect, the ethnic communities surrounding them.

Theological foundation of Christian multiculturalism

The theology of the church is arguably a theology of inclusivity, reconciliation, and oneness. According to this theology, a functional church will need to blend its ecclesiology and missiology, making them two sides of the same coin. Organizationally, there will have to be a systemic approach to church development and a structure to facilitate a local church's organismic operation, with an eventual goal of the final joining of God's peoples in the heavenly reunion with the Triune God and His angelic hosts.

---

[24] Enoch Wan's proposed guideline for biblical exegesis states that in order for a biblical precedent or verse to be universally valid, it needs to be in agreement with the following five steps: scripturally based, theologically sound, theoretically coherent, contextually relevant, and practically applicable. See Appendix 1.

The Mystery of Christ

In his letter to the Ephesians, Paul describes a personal experience through which a revelation was given him regarding the nature of the church. He first calls it "the mystery of Christ" (3:2-4). "This mystery is that through the gospel the Gentiles are heirs together with Israel, members together of one body, and sharers together in the promise in Christ Jesus" (3:6). Mark DeYmaz calls this the Pauline Mystery in his landmark book on the Multiethnic Church.[25] Paul calls this "the mystery hidden to generations before and now in Christ is revealed to the world." The Church, as a subsequent embodiment of this new person in Christ, serves as a testament and witness to the world. We have the letter to the Ephesians that most vividly describes this (3:2-11). Paul wrote about this uncovering of mystery with such an excitement that he felt a total sense of unworthiness to be the repository of such a profound revelation. As a servant of God's grace, Paul was suffering personally for such a great work done through Christ for humanity. DeYmaz points out that it was for this reason Paul was actually imprisoned.[26] This complete reconciliation and restoration of relationships, both vertical and horizontal, is an awe-inspiring statement to the rulers and authorities in the heavenly realms.

Relationship between the Mystery of Christ and the Church

The Mystery of Christ not only is the message Paul commits his life to sharing, he also tells us that the church is the embodiment and the realizing ground for this truth. As heirs, members of one body, and sharers together in the promise in Christ Jesus (Eph. 3:6), the members of a local church must make every effort to keep the unity of the Spirit through the bond of peace (Eph. 4:1-3). God intends for the church to demonstrate His wisdom to even the rulers and authorities in the heavenly realms. The church is God's agent of change to the fallen state of the world, which the principalities of the heavenly realms have been observing for as long as there has been humanity. More than anybody, they are eager and curious about what is going to be the answer to this human plight. The Apostle Peter also mentioned that the angels desire to see into these things (1 Peter 1:12). For the fallen rulers and principalities who may delight over the temptation and the fall of humanity, they too must be shocked to see that God through His Son Jesus Christ has brought about forgiveness and redemption for the world, and that through the church, peoples of various backgrounds are coming together to show the devil that his scheme is destroyed and he is defeated (1 John 3:8). When Christians live in harmony with people from different backgrounds, there is true victory. The coming of the Holy Spirit on the day of Pentecost brought the church into being. The gift of tongues serves, among its other purposes, as a sign of the unity that the Spirit of God brings to His church.

Multiculturalism and Multiethnic Ministries

Entering the 21st century, the world was hurled into chaos, a multifaceted confusion of ethnic strife, cultural war, people movements, ideological morass, religious extremism, terrorism, financial

---

[25] DeYmaz, Building A Healthy Multiethnic Church, 27.
[26] DeYmaz, Building A Healthy Multiethnic Church, 31.

meltdown, and yes, natural calamities. After 9/11 all hell broke loose on a global scale. This research is not about apocalyptic forecast. Nor is it about the prediction of the second coming of Christ. However, all the phenomena of the 21st century seem to be vividly reflective of the prophecy by Christ about the end times (Matthew 24). This may be the darkest of times, yet it is, nonetheless, the brightest of times. There has never been a time such as this when the gospel of Jesus Christ is reaching every corner of the world. This is the time for a reasserted push for the end time ultimate reconciliation of all peoples through Jesus Christ, the Prince of Peace. Evangelism is the means, and the message is Christ, the ultimate Peacemaker, bringing all peoples of the Church to the household of God, of which Christ is the Chief Cornerstone. The churches of Jesus Christ, thus are the embassy and consulate of the Kingdom of God on earth, making a statement to the world both visible and invisible that the wisdom of God (the cross and Christ crucified) is triumphant over the wisdom of the world. Every local church is a beachhead on the shore of the enemy's territory, a dagger stabbed right in the heart of the devil. He knows his days are numbered, hence the chaos, the confusion, and the clashes. Of course the world has its own brand of remedies for all its ills. For terrorism, we have military machines; for economic woes, we have the big bailout; for disasters, we have humanitarian aid, and to a post-modern pluralistic and ethnically diverse society with all its relativism and experientialism, we hear about progressive secularism and multiculturalism. What then is the church's message for our time that will point toward the direction of hope and, yes, salvation?

Toward A Christian Multiculturalism

The secular sense of the word "multiculturalism" is loaded with confusing and conflicting concepts, which, when not clearly discerned, can lead to relativism.[27] The proposal here is that the church has a Christian multiculturalism that is biblically based, theologically sound, contextually relevant, culturally sensitive, and timely. However, most churches and Christian literature have not been laser sharp enough to show the confused world out there the way to Christ our eternal Savior. His work and life is the answer to our woes. Christian Multiculturalism is the Christian message for our time. Based on the biblical foundation and theological understanding here developed, we can now define the concept of Christian Multiculturalism and its implications for Christian communication, ministry, and missions in an ethnically diverse and multicultural society.

Secular Multiculturalism

Multiculturalism is a concept promoted by governments and academia as the fundamental ideology for a multiethnic, pluralistic society.[28] It is adopted by countries that embrace immigration and welcome cultural diversity. Countries like Canada, Australia, most western European nations and, by and large, the United States, all have multiculturalism as the basic ethos for policies regarding ethnic diversity and cultural pluralism. Multiculturalism seeks to provide answers to the problems of racism, discrimination, ethnic harmony and equality, immigration issues and political equity. Its goal

---

[27] Manuel Ortiz, *One New People: Models for Developing a Multiethnic Church*. (Downers Grove, IL: Intervarsity Press, 1996), 467-470.
[28] Immigrant countries like Canada, adopted a policy of multiculturalism which seeks to recognize the reality of pluralism in the country. In this mode of thinking, instead of assimilation, the government of Canada encourages all Canadians to cultural pluralism. For details read: *Multiculturalism in Canada*.
<http://www.mta.ca/about_canada/mlti/> 09.19.12.

is to create a pluralistic society where all cultures, ethnic groups, ideologies, and lifestyles are accepted and respected by all members of society. The ideal is that all people will live harmoniously, i.e., to live and let live. Tolerance, in this sense, is the core value for multiculturalism. Multiculturalism with a liberal agenda seeks to silence all voices that promote absolute and universal truth, particularly that of a religious conviction. However, if one seeks to dissect this secular ideal of multiculturalism, one finds that at the core of its belief system is tolerance without foundation. It is merely an ideal, wishful thinking given utterance. No one can tolerate a terrorist whose sole aim is to kill anyone regarded as an infidel. Tolerance in the face of a violent fundamentalist becomes completely pale and speechless. There will be victims but no martyrs for the cause of multiculturalism. The very essence of multiculturalism is formed around the equality and equal validity of all cultural norms, beliefs, and practices. And culture, to a secular multiculturalist, naturally includes faith and religious beliefs. This is the blind spot of secular multiculturalism and where it loses its power to congeal. Since secular multiculturalism by itself has no absolutes, nobody will lay down their life for such an empty concept. It may echo well with the trend of a postmodern society, which trumpets relativism, but it has no convictions. Secular multiculturalism can only harass non-violent ideologues, like most fundamental and evangelical Christians, but will easily succumb and be rendered powerless to violent bullies. However, Christians with their faith based on the death and resurrection of Jesus Christ, a Great Commission to make disciples of the world, bring them into the fold of the family of God, have a conviction for which they are willing to lay down their lives. They may be victims of violence, yet they are willing messengers of love and peace. Throughout the two thousand years of Christian missions Christ and His disciples bear testimony to this conviction and its transforming power. This is what separates the Christian message from secular multiculturalism.

Biblical Foundation of Christian Multiculturalism

If the secular world seeks to build a society with diverse ethnic and cultural groups co-existing harmoniously with one another, Christians seek to reach out to and be united with all peoples of the world. Through this effort, barriers are destroyed and walls of hostility torn down (Eph. 2:14-15). Through service, witness, and persuasion, Christians seek to share the message and the person of Jesus Christ, the ultimate Peacemaker of peoples and God, the Creator. This basic message of the gospel may have been waylaid, misunderstood, or misrepresented, but it never changes its core: Christ and Him crucified, which is the embodiment of love, forgiveness, and grace.

Theological Foundation of Christian Multiculturalism

The theological foundation for Christian Multiculturalism is firmly based on the completed works of Jesus Christ. Ephesians 2:16 spells out clearly that the purpose of Christ's salvific work is not merely evangelism but the formation of a new community called the church which in essence should be multiethnic bridging cultural, socio-economic, and gender barriers. "His purpose was to create in Himself one new man out of the two, thus making peace, and in this one body to reconcile both of them to God through the cross, by which He put to death their hostility" (Eph. 2:16-17). Unity in Christ, therefore, is the end of Christian mission so that the Bride may be presented to the Bridegroom on that day of the heavenly wedding of the Lamb (Rev. 19:7). This theology of oneness is the message the Christian church should be focusing on in her proclamation, demonstration, and impartation to the world that desperately seeks answers through all its failed and pale attempts of human-based multiculturalism. The world remains divided. They not only need a savior, Jesus, they need the Prince of Peace, Jesus as their Chief Cornerstone for a truly unified world community.

The Mystery of Christ Revealed

In Ephesians 3:6, Paul described a very significant revelation he received from God (which is theological because it was through a direct inspiration) about a mystery of Christ that was hidden before. This mystery now, as it is revealed, presents a revolutionary view of the true heart of God.[29] "This mystery is that through the gospel the Gentiles are heirs together with Israel, members together of one body, and sharers together in the promise in Christ Jesus"(Eph. 3:6).

All peoples of the world are to be united through Christ Jesus in one body and in the promise in Christ Jesus. Paul was so excited about this revelation he received that he called it "the unsearchable riches of Christ." He also could not contain his sense of honor to be able to make the mystery of Christ known to all to whom he came to preach the good news. This is far more than evangelism; this is a total transformation of the human race back to the fold of Christ. This is the theological foundation for Christian multiculturalism that embraces all through faith in Jesus Christ.

The Church as Embassy of the Kingdom of God on Earth

Paul saw, in Ephesians 3:10-12, that God has a unique role for His church on earth, which is to demonstrate the manifold wisdom of God to even the rulers and authorities in the heavenly realms. What does the church have to offer, that even the angelic beings are to be told and shown, of God's eternal plan of unity through His Son Jesus Christ? What did God want to demonstrate to the angelic beings, both faithful and fallen, through the church? From this passage we can see there are at least two main reasons. First, God wanted to show to the angels, who witnessed the separation of the human race from their Maker and the subsequent division of mankind, the reuniting of the human race through Jesus Christ. This is the ultimate relational restoration both between humanity and God, and among the human race itself. This is definitely headline news among the angels. Second, God wanted to show to the devil and his cohorts that God is using His church to shame them and to destroy their work. The Church of Jesus Christ, therefore, is the embodiment of this message of multiethnic union. The authorities in the heavenly realms are naturally shocked and amazed at the wisdom of God. Unity in Christ is truly the most important message to send to the world by Christ's Church.

Structures for Multiethnic Churches

In practical terms, to set up the structure to accommodate the inclusion of various ethnic groups in one church requires more than merely good theology and intention. Many churches may have both of the above, yet lack the necessary organizational framework to allow a multiethnic body to blend and grow. Many organizational models have been used by churches for various reasons, such as the demographics of the community, key leaders' backgrounds and preferences, practical arrangements

---

[29] DeYmaz, Building a Healthy Multiethnic Church, 30.

to house the ethnic groups, leadership structures, programs, and other methods of inclusion. Some have promoted one over others and claim a biblical mandate for such. Typically, one finds that the key leaders' vision determines the choice of organizational structure. One also finds that it is a journey of fine-tuning and restructuring as the leadership matures and learns through trials and mistakes, seeking to find a balance between church as a functioning body and church as a cooperative social model. There is also this dimension of avoiding economic inequality between cooperating communities in maintaining expensive facilities and programs through a multiethnic church operation.

By definition, a multiethnic church is a church where more than one ethnic group is found. In today's North American context, most churches will have more than one ethnic group represented in their congregation. So, to define a church as multiethnic, one needs to find more than a handful of people from other ethnic groups differing from the main body to have enough representation in the church to make the term meaningful.

Among the studies on this subject which I gathered, all subscribe to a 20 percent threshold for such a designation. That is, to be a meaningful multiethnic church, 20 percent of the church members must be from a different ethnic background than the majority. How did such a percentage come to be adopted? Michael O. Emerson claims that this percentage is not merely arbitrary. He quoted Rosebeth Kanter's study on the effects of proportions on group life and said that "at this percentage, the proportion is high enough to have its presence felt and filtered throughout a system or organization." Emerson also claims that his personal studies on this subject agree with Kanter's finding.[30] At 20 percent, an ethnic group's presence will be noticeable. Emerson further estimates from his findings, that in North America, according to such a definition, "seven percent of American congregations are multiracial."[31] Among them, most are Anglo majority churches with other ethnic groups among them. After analyzing several organizational structures adopted by some multiethnic churches and understanding their rationales for their structures, we will propose some principles for churches desiring to morph into multiethnic churches.

In today's multiethnic setting, doing church and doing missions are concentric circles of the same multiethnic fabric that extend from one church's community to the world at large. Missions in this sense becomes a natural extension of what a church is and does locally. This development is called sociological glocalization by economists. In this light, a local church's cross-cultural ministry is not exclusively about missions, rather, who we are as a church, and how we bring the Kingdom of God to the world as the church, through which "the manifold wisdom of God should be made known to the rulers and authorities in the heavenly realms" (Eph. 3:10). This situation may be viewed from a diaspora missiological perspective, since diaspora missions is also a related development in the missiological circle and in world evangelization. So to engage the church in formulating such a model, I have worked on developing a church model which is scripturally based, theologically sound, theoretically viable, organizationally functional, and culturally relevant.

The majority of churches in Taiwan need to respond to this increasingly diverse and multiethnic reality of the cities regardless of their feelings. With such a background, I seek to engage the stakeholders in this church to develop multilingual congregations in Wu Chang Church. It is a model

---

[30] Michael O. Emerson, *People of the Dream: Multiracial Congregations in the United States*, (New Jersey: Princeton University Press, 2006), 35.
[31] Emerson, 36.

that seeks to put into practice the idea of homogeneity within heterogeneity and unity in diversity. Putting the multiethnic church paradigm under the light of diaspora missiology, multiethnic church offers local churches options to take advantage of the changing demographics around them and to build themselves up to be churches that seek to live out the metaphor of the One New Person Paul describes.

Many practitioners of multiethnic churches describe how their churches grew in their pursuit of such a vision and how in the process they developed and fine-tuned their structures to accommodate their vision and development. Rodney M. Woo, author of *The Color of Church* and senior pastor of the Wilcrest Baptist Church, whose name and church were also quoted in Emerson's *People of the Dream*, said that when he first joined the church, there were two distinctive congregations, the sponsoring white and the Chinese mission congregation, between which there was not much interaction. There was also an African-American mission. For Woo, the multiple congregational model of Wilcrest was not truly multiethnic, though it gave that impression.[32] The three congregations basically did not have ministry interactions among themselves. Through worship and leadership restructuring, he guided the church to be an English medium congregation with multiple ethnic groups represented. Emerson describes his journey with Mosaic Church in Little Rock as a path from unintended exclusion to graduated inclusion.[33] In this process, Woo's approach gives the first generation immigrants, where culture and languages make it hard to be part of the multiethnic blend, over to their respective ethnic churches, while DeYmaz tries to keep them together using a model for inclusion suggested by a pastor friend, David Uth. The model is essentially a gradual approach to incorporate various ethnic groups through language specific cell groups and then further move toward a multiethnic worship.[34] Both of these models reach certain cross sections of the multiethnic community of these churches, and due to the lack of culture and language competency, that is where their churches will remain. Ortiz, in his description of the various multiethnic church models, is more relaxed and descriptive in his study of this phenomenon, understandably so because it was written from an academic researcher's perspective. Ortiz makes a distinction between multi-congregational churches and multiethnic churches.[35] The dividing line still lies in language. A multi-congregational church is a church with several ethnic/language-specific congregations worshipping under the same roof or which fall under the same leadership structure. A multiethnic church in America is an English-medium worship with multiple ethnic groups. Taking the biblical churches as examples, we can compare DeYmaz's Mosaic Church to that of the Jerusalem church, where there was at least one non-Hebrew (Greek) speaking sub-group existing within the larger body, whereas Woo's church is more comparable to the Antioch church, which is more of a Greek-speaking Gentile church with multiple bicultural leaders such as Barnabas and Paul among the leadership. All of these mentioned are examples of working cases of successful inter-ethnic congregations and pastoral staff.

---

[32] Rodney M. Woo, *The Color of Church: A Biblical and Practical Paradigm for Multiracial Churches*, (Nashville, Tennessee: B&H Publishing Group, 2009), 1511-1515.
[33] DeYmaz, *Ethnic Blends*, 111.
[34] DeYmaz, *Ethnic Blends*, 108.
[35] Ortiz, One New People, 63.

Tackling Barriers to Multiethnic Development

To develop a multiethnic church either from scratch or from a mono-ethnic church, the lead pastor has several barriers to tackle. The first and most challenging is ethnocentrism. Ethnocentrism is defined as "the practice of interpreting and evaluating behavior and objects by reference to the standards of one's own culture rather than by those of the culture to which they belong."[36] Ethnocentrism in and of itself may not be morally wrong. It is simply a way of viewing the world in terms of one's own culture.[37] Yet when it goes unchecked it has a tendency to cause a group of people to evaluate other cultures using their own as the yardstick, which will lead to the belief that one's culture is superior to another's culture.[38] That people tend to measure other ethnic groups and cultures in relation to their own is human nature. It is both inward looking and outward shunning. Ethnocentrism causes one ethnic group in a multiethnic environment to look inward to protect their interests, values, traditions, customs, and way of life. Ethnocentrism makes people use their cultures to measure other ethnic groups and pass moral judgment on what they observe in other ethnic groups. The results are often generalization and stereotyping which lead to prejudices. To address this tendency, most anthropologists propose using cultural relativism.

The second barrier to multiethnic development within a church is racial prejudice.[39] Racial prejudice or racism is the negative outcome of commonly accepted stereotypes of one ethnic group or culture by another. It is "the assumption of one's own racial superiority and the arrogance and behavior patterns that accompany that assumption."[40] The result of racial prejudice as played out in a multiethnic environment, is that the dominate ethnic group will use its power to force conformity on other minority groups and the minorities will in turn huddle together to seek protection from the other side. It may require the speaking of the dominant group's language through legal means and education to avoid such a problem; otherwise the result is the alignments along ethnic lines that we see in a multiethnic society today. However, the presence of the church is to break down these walls, therefore, a relational theology and intentionality of Christian leaders will help their churches bridge the gaps in between these groups and ease the ethnic tension among them. The eventual goal is to allow the groups to come together and see a higher commonality among them, which is their identity as the children of God, the true meaning of Christians.

The third invisible barrier for multiethnic church development is more subtle but pervasive in all churches. Donald McGavran's Homogeneous Unit Principle (HUP),[41] which was applied by the American Church Growth Movement, remains the *Modus Operandi* for most churches today. Not only has this principle provided guidance for church development for pastors in the last thirty years in evangelical churches, it gives directive to the structuring of church as part of the remnant of the church growth movement since the 70s. As described in the theology for multiethnic church, the HUP

---

[36] Stephen A. Grunlan and Marvin K. Mayers, Cultural Anthropology: A Christian Perspective, 2nd Edition. (Grand Rapids, MI: Zondervan, 1988), 24.
[37] Grunlan and K. Mayers, Cultural Anthropology, 24.
[38] DeYmaz, Building A Healthy Multiethnic Church, 101.
[39] The author's preference for choosing the word "ethnic" over "racial" is evident in his writing, however, here the author is using a commonly accepted term to describe a phenomenon. To the author ethnic is a more accurate and suitable term than racial in this research.
[40] Grunlan and Mayers, *Cultural Anthropology*, 131.
[41] Donald A. McGavran, *Understanding Church Growth*, 2nd Edition, (Grand Rapids, MI, Wm. B. Eerdmans Publishing Co. 1990), 178.

gives legitimacy for churches to exclude other ethnic and social groups for the sake of church growth. This is a highly functional and goal-oriented approach to church ministry. Yet in this process of pursuing growth, it undercuts the very essence of what a church is meant to be, a reconciled community with their Creator and among themselves. "For in Christ, there is neither Jew nor Greek, slave nor free, male nor female, for you are all one in Christ Jesus" (Gal. 3:28). To help break this old barrier, pastors and key leaders of the church need to be reeducated about what church is scripturally and how to develop it in today's multiethnic environment. It will take many steps to educate the church body about the true meaning of church and the heart of the Father. Such change can only come through incremental steps, for people's hearts and minds take a long time to change. And the church growth model, though rarely talked about today in America, is still the underlying paradigm for church development and ministry. This principle helps shape many churches' organizational structures, worship, and ministries. It fortifies the justification of the dominant ethnic group. Such structure, from the leadership to church operations, serves as the old wineskin, so even if the key leader's mindset is challenged by a multiethnic paradigm, the existing structure will not allow the church to make any meaningful change. Therefore, for a church to grow into a multiethnic church, there needs to be a new wineskin.

Leadership Structure

All great works begin with one person. A brave and committed leader is the key to the transformation and development of a multiethnic church. Without exception pastors who shared about their journeys toward multiethnic ministries, always shared about a strong, nearly revelatory calling to this endeavor. DeYmaz looked at his work more from a racial reconciliation point of view, especially in the place of his calling—Arkansas with its southern history.[42] Woo came to this vision more from his personal multiethnic heritage and the subsequent burden to see the coming together of God's people in His church.[43] Leadership structure is set up for dual purposes. First it needs to allow the key leader and the leadership team to address barriers toward a multiethnic church body. Second, the structure must be able to allow the multiethnic body to function in such a way that all ethnic groups find their footing in this big body, and at the same time learn to appreciate one another and work together toward a gradual blending aiming at the heavenly coming together of people from every nation, tribe, people, and language standing, before the throne, in front of the Lamb (Rev. 7:9).

Multiethnic Leadership

Ortiz and others believe that, second to a visionary leader to trumpet such a multiethnic effort, the next element needed is a multiethnic leadership team.[44] Woo mentioned how he invited a black youth pastor to join his staff. Yancey believes that a multiethnic leadership structure needs to be intentionally created.[45] The reasons are obvious—the congregation wants to see their own ethnic leaders represented in the leadership of the church. Also, for outreach purposes, having ethnic pastors

---

[42] DeYmaz, Building A Healthy Multiethnic Church, 1.
[43] Woo, The Color of Church, 4.
[44] Ortiz, One New People, 58.
[45] George Yancey, One Body, One Spirit: Principles of Successful Multiracial Churches, (Downers Grove, IL: Intervarsity Press, 2003), 86.

on board tells the community the church is serious about meeting their needs. On the flip side, if the leadership "lacks representation from a particular segment of the church, its decisions are more likely to be criticized and second-guessed as biased or unfair."[46] Yancey also points out that with a multiethnic staff, the worship and program design can better reflect the multicultural expression of worship. All of these contribute to the inclusion of ethnic groups in this larger body. The presence and practice of multiethnicity in the church not only address the needs of the congregation, it will also create a new culture with this diverse body and, over time, people, especially those who become believers in this kind of church, will take this multiethnic display as a given. At my church in the U.S., our first move toward multiethnic staff was to invite a white youth pastor to lead this predominately Chinese-American youth group. Different from other ethnic Chinese churches in North America that also have invited white youth pastors, Galilee South Community Church invited this youth pastor not with a job description to pastor the Chinese kids but to serve and develop the English-speaking youth, no matter what their ethnic backgrounds. On the flip side, Yancey also cautions that even though we need to be intentional about creating a multiethnic leadership, the focus should not be to meet a quota or to invite someone who is not qualified or theologically compatible.[47]

Multi-congregational/Multiethnic Church

There are various models for multi-congregational/multiethnic church development which Ortiz lists[48] with two basic types.[49] For urban areas such as New York City, where virtually all of the world's major ethnic groups and immigrant communities are co-existing alongside one another, and where real estate is hard to find and nearly impossible for some to acquire, sharing a common facility seems a logical and natural way to go. Therefore, multi-congregational churches like the First Baptist Church of Flushing and First Church of the Nazarene of Los Angeles came to be.[50] Ortiz among others defines a multi-congregational church as:

...a church that has taken on the challenge of biblical justice and missions in the context of racial strife and increased pluralism. It builds relationships between the different language groups, intent on bringing biblical reconciliation between them. This display of the kingdom of God motivates Multilanguage congregations to come together and to restructure the present monocultural formation of the church into one that is based on obedience to the Word of God. The multi-congregational church provides for both autonomy and interdependency.[51]

This definition given by Ortiz is meaningful for the following reasons. First it points out that language, more than other factors, keeps these congregations separate. It takes a person with a bi-cultural/lingual background to appreciate the enormous gap that is created by language and cultures. Within this multi-congregational model, there are still variants. There is this renting and hosting

---

[46] Jim Herrington, Mike Bonem and James H. Furr. *Leading Congregational Change: A Practical Guide for The Transfromational Journey*, (San Francisco, CA: Jossey-Bass Publishers, 2000), 45.
[47] Yancey, One Body, One Spirit, 96.
[48] Manuel Ortiz differentiates multi-congregational church models from multiethnic church models. For this research, I do not differentiate between the two. For me, these are multiethnic churches in various forms and levels of integration. See: Ortiz, One New People, Models for Developing A Multiethnic Church. (Downers Grove, IL: Intervarsity Press, 1996).
[49] Ortiz, One New People, 497-499.
[50] Ortiz, One New People, 514-517.
[51] Ortiz, *One New People*, 517-520.

church relationship, where a hosting church, which is of one ethnic group, owns and operates the building and leases part of the building out to one or more ethnic congregations. Their organizations remain separate, although with occasional joint activities. There is also another multi-congregational church that is more integrated. The congregations belong to the same church organization, share the same facility, and have the same budget, church vision, and philosophy of ministry.[52] Second, the provision for both autonomy and interdependency is profound. Some think that if we have a church with all the ethnic groups joining the dominant ethnic group that generally means that all ethnic groups become part of an English-speaking white congregation. This holds true especially in America. This is not a multiethnic church, rather a forced integration since there is no regard for language or cultural differences, especially those of the first generation immigrants. Any serious multiethnic church endeavor will eventually have to come to terms with the need for language and cultural preferences by the first generation immigrants, unless a multiethnic church decides that is not the segment of demographics to include. In so doing, the church simply gives the need or problem to the ethnic churches in the same community and only targets their second generation. Ethnic churches can exist in multiethnic societies like America if all the congregants have a sense of belonging, feel safe and at ease. Every ethnic group needs their autonomy. However, a multi-congregational church wants to meet this need yet does not simply want to stay there. It sees the greater biblical mandate for bringing all ethnic groups together, where they can learn to appreciate each other, to depend on each other, and thrive. So in a multi-congregational church, as Ortiz defines it, believers from various ethnic backgrounds can enjoy their homogeneity as well as celebrate their heterogeneity.

Homogeneity within Heterogeneity

How can a church structure itself to accomplish such goals? Maintaining homogeneity and celebrating heterogeneity, at times, seems like trying to mix water with oil. However, from the Jerusalem church model, we see that at least two language groups can co-exist within one church and grow together despite their challenges. Good things can come through such challenges. For the Jerusalem church, the complaint brought to the disciples about the inequality of food distribution between the Hebrew and the Greek speaking groups highlighted a need for better management and job descriptions for leaders as the church grew. This led to developing qualifications for deacons, and leaders were chosen to meet this need. The disciples focused more on prayer and teaching the word, and the deacons met the daily operational needs of the church. Such is the organization framework for most churches today. Let us be reminded that it was out of a challenge along these ethnic lines that a greater resolution was found. The disciples did not choose to tell the Greek-speaking group to form their own church as a homogeneous unit. They maintained the unity of the body of Christ and as a result the church members were satisfied and the church continued to grow (Acts 6:1-7).

Cell Group Model for Multiethnic Ministries

Cell Group Model answers people's cry for relationship rather than rituals; it corresponds to the biblical mandate for unity rather than division. This is a picture of a church that is obedient to both the Great Commission and the Great Commandment. Planting homogeneous cell groups is a strategic

---

[52] Ortiz, One New People, 514-517.

church growth model. It is an answer to the cry for relevancy in church life, a need to get back to a relational rather than merely a ritual Christianity as found in more traditional churches. It springs from a re-examination of the traditional clergy-led, hierarchical church institution and seeks to return to a biblical model of church living. Similarly, the house church movement aims to address the problem of a lack of meaningful relationships in the body of Christ. On the other hand, in terms of missions, which is not merely geographical but cultural, churches today are largely too inward-looking to see what their communities are becoming. The world has come to the cities, not merely in the Western world but all across the globe. This is the age of cyberspace, internal migrations, and economic globalization.

For most churches today, the Homogeneous Unit Principle continues to (often unconsciously) dominate thinking on church development and missions. Important as this is, however, the larger context of multicultural and rapidly-globalized communities presents a bigger challenge and opportunity for churches today to become relevant again. House churches and people group approaches to church building are only half the answer. The other half is hidden in the answer to these questions: How should a church in this cyber-age and global village answer the cry for relevancy in terms of spiritual needs and ethnic and racial relations? Is there a church model for the 21st century that will satisfy both the spiritual void of the age of relativism and the cry of unity in societies like that of Taiwan? I believe there is, and the answer lies in the Bible. Examples are right there before our eyes in the record of the Acts of the Apostles. The mandate is there, too. The biblical precedents are there, as well as a picture of what this church model will look like, revealed in the realized church of the Kingdom of God in the book of Revelation, where the redeemed from all nations, tongues, and tribes gather before the throne of God as one body. So our challenge is this: Do we dare to let the Bible once again take authority over our thinking, our values, our practice, and our mission? The answer is what I aim to present here: A cell-group based, multiethnic church that seeks to satisfy the need for relationship and fulfillment in a church body, while at the same time striving "to maintain the unity of the Spirit" (Eph. 4:1-3) in a diverse body of Christ amid all the cultural, ethnic, and linguistic diversity we find in today's urban world.

Summary

In a multiethnic society, the line between the mission (local) and missions (foreign) for a church is becoming more and more blurry. I believe a re-examination of the whole concept of and correlation between the church (ecclesiology) and her mission (missiology) is needed. There needs to be a re-examination of the biblical foundation for the Church and a review of Christian missions history, particularly in culturally and ethnically diverse settings where missionary cultures were not regarded as superior to the recipient cultures. Secondly, there must be insights drawn from cultural anthropology, and particularly sociology, to see how cultures interact in an urban community and how this interaction affects the operation of the local churches and their mission. Finally, it is imperative to take action with a new missions paradigm in mind for a church to conduct its mission in a multiethnic context. This new paradigm must be based strongly on the concept that a church should have representation that resembles the makeup of the community—otherwise; it is not fulfilling her mandate. The theology of ecclesiology is a theology inclusive of diversity, which is the very nature of the church.

I also re-examine McGavran's Homogeneous Unit Principle (HUP) traditionally taken as a formula for church growth, making what was intended to be descriptive, prescriptive. The resulting furtherance of divisions in the body of Christ and waste of resources outweigh the benefit of growth from following the HUP, particularly in an ethnically diverse society. Equality among cultures has been theoretically discussed in modern missions scholarship, but it has resulted by and large in an intellectual understanding, not a conviction that impacts the way missions is done. This emphasis should be seen being worked out at both the Christian academia and practical ministry levels, both of which I address.

CHAPTER 4

MULTIETHNIC MINISTRY OF

THE WU CHANG CHURCH

Introduction

When I began to lay out my research questions, I had in my mind a clear purpose to find out all the relevant facts and information about the state of the Wu Chang Church and, through research, to incrementally nudge the church toward a multiethnic model, which I strongly believe to be the kind of church one reads about in the scriptural records, and the ideal church prophetically revealed in Pauline theology. I added his critique of what I observed to be "wishful thinking"—the multiculturalism adopted by the government as the prescription for the challenges and ills of the multiethnic society of Taiwan. The second critique I had was of the guiding principle of Homogenous Unit Principle as the church growth doctrine for organization and operation. To respond, I proposed a Christian version of multiculturalism, which is based on the completed work of the Son of God, Jesus and His cross. I also proposed that a multiethnic church will be a beautiful testimony and a hope for the nations in this globalized society. What's more, this model is practical and adaptable, with more and more churches around the world adopting it. I applied my assumptions and study on an actual church in a real context, i.e. the Wu Chang Church in Kaohsiung. I propose that a multiethnic church is even more fitting for today's multiethnic societies around the world of which Taiwan is a part. In this chapter we report the findings through surveys, participant observations, in-depth interviews, and, most of all, the actions taken. All of the information presented is for the Wu Chang Church to rally herself for the future mission God has for her.

Survey of Wu Chang Church Membership and Ethnic Makeup of the Wu Chang Church

Survey: Wu Chang Church Membership

The survey of August 26, 2012 was analyzed to show the following distribution and level of interest pertaining to the topic of multiethnic ministry of the Wu Chang Church. A total of 1000 copies of the survey were distributed on that Sunday to three congregations--one Taiwanese and two Mandarin services. The same survey was posted on Facebook for the Wu Chang Church's young adult and bilingual fellowships. The members were told that this is a study of the church member's level of understanding and interest of multiethnic ministry, which might explain why the returned finished copies were only 1/5 of the total copies. This may be interpreted as showing the general indifference of the members to this issue. By the time we closed the survey entry on the internet and collected all finished hard copies, there were a total of 199 valid surveys. I exported the online survey to an Excel document, which was later arranged and data quantified to produce the following graphs. We will explain the findings these graphs reveal about the church's take on multiethnic ministry. The findings through this survey will be based on the data collected from these valid copies. The title of the survey was called, "A Survey on Wu Chang Church's Awareness and Interest of Multiethnic Ministry."[53]

The first data I sought regarding the Wu Chang Church is the ethnic makeup of her membership (Figure 1). From the returned surveys, we find that 1.0% belong to New Residents, which are the

Wuchang Church Ethnicity Distribution

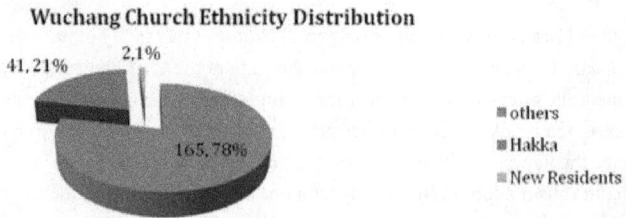

41,21%   2,1%

165,78%

■ others
■ Hakka
■ New Residents

people of foreign descent who are here permanently. A total of 21% identified themselves as Hakka or have partial Hakka blood in them. The majority of the respondents identified themselves in the category called "others," which in the Wu Chang Church's context means they belong to the following three ethnic groups, the native tribal groups, the Minnan or the mainlanders.

Figure 1

Ethnic Makeup of the Wu Chang Church

I put the three groups in the category called "others" to avoid unnecessary misunderstanding that I was trying to divide the church members according to their ethnic background. This is a very sensitive topic for people in Taiwan, especially in the south. Another reason was that all of the Minnan speaking people in the church already have a Minnan service to attend and the tribal groups living in the city are assimilated into the Mandarin-speaking majority of the population, therefore no city churches in Kaohsiung offer tribal language services. Even in the mountainous tribal regions, many of the church services are conducted in Mandarin.

---

[53] See Appendix 4.

The last and most important reason why I only designed the survey to show the Hakka and New Residents groups in this church is because in the last year, this church has been calling for outreach to the Hakka and New Residents; therefore, it is quite natural for church members to respond to this survey without feeling singled out. From this initial survey, I discovered that the church has a sizable percentage of people who are Hakka. These Hakka may have lived in the city for generations. On the surface, there is no observable way to recognize they are Hakka; however, a strong ethnic identity still exists among these people. The number of New Residents who responded from this survey only takes up 1% of the total respondents. This means that the entire number of New Residents in this church is still small. I discovered that most of the New Residents did not take part in this survey, some because they do not read Chinese, and some because they do not want to reveal their backgrounds, especially spouses from the mainland of China. They prefer to live anonymously among us. Those who responded were Malaysian Chinese who have lived in Taiwan for over 15 years. They still speak Mandarin with an accent, though they are more comfortable letting people know where they are from.

The survey questioned the respondents about whether they employ foreign caretakers/caregivers in their homes typically for caring for the disabled senior and handicapped family members (Figure 2). The government sets a high bar for employment of foreign workers at home for individual purposes. Yet even with such restrictions, a good 11% of the respondents reported having foreign caretakers/caregivers in their homes. This can be interpreted in two ways or a combination of both. The first is that the respondents did the survey because they are more aware of the multiethnic reality around them. The second is that for the metro area where Wu Chang Church is located, there is a higher percentage of elderly people; therefore, the need for foreign workers is higher. However, regardless of the reason, this 11% shows that for this church, the care and ministry toward the foreign workers in the home is a valid and necessary work that needs to be developed. With regard to these homes, the graph in Figure 3 shows where these foreign workers come from.

Do you employ foreign caretakers for your house or business?

⊟ Yes ⊟ No

22,11%

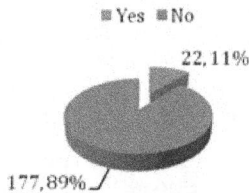

177,89%

Figure 2

Employment of Foreign Caretakers/Caregivers in Home or Business

The caretakers/caregivers who come from Indonesia are 77% of the total, presumably mostly of Muslim background (Figure 3). Then 18% come from the Philippines and 5% from Vietnam. This finding shows that there is a big need for Indonesian ministry among the foreign workers. During the September 30 Community Sunday service, the church prepared a number of Indonesian language evangelistic tracks and brochures along with gifts for these caretakers/caregivers from Indonesia.

For Filipino caretakers, there is the possibility of partnering with the CB Association of the Philippines to come up with ways to reach out to them. I visited Indonesia twice during my research period. A church from Bandung, Indonesia comes to Kaohsiung to give a worship conference each spring. The senior pastor of the Wu Chang Church, Rev. John Cheng, has a plan to undertake a partnership with that church for missionary work in Indonesia. The other possibility, as this survey shows, is for the Indonesian church to consider doing work in Kaohsiung among the Indonesians.

Countries of origin for foreign caretakers in Wuchchang church

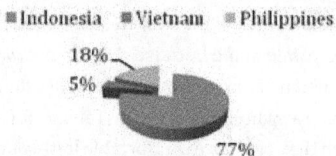

▪ Indonesia ▪ Vietnam ▪ Philippines

18%
5%
77%

Figure 3

Foreign Caretakers/Caregivers' Countries of Origin

Among the 199 respondents, 103 fully agreed to support and get involved in the church's outreach to New Residents (Figure 4). This is a positive indication, because this says that this church has a large number of people who are willing to get involved to be part of the outreach programs, and care for either foreign spouses or foreign workers. I communicated this information to the board and executive secretary of the Community Care Association of the Wu Chang Church. The board included a ministry to the New Residents as one of the three major thrusts of the association's 2013 goals. The plan is to provide home visits to senior people as well as to foreign caretakers/caregivers. Another plan is to visit caretakers/caregivers in two parks near the church where they congregate when bringing disabled patients out for fresh air. There is additionally a plan to recruit Indonesian and English speaking volunteers to form teams and train people to conduct outreach to this new group of people among us.

Figure 4

Support and Involvement in Outreach to New Residents

Do you want to support and involve in the church's outreach to new residents?

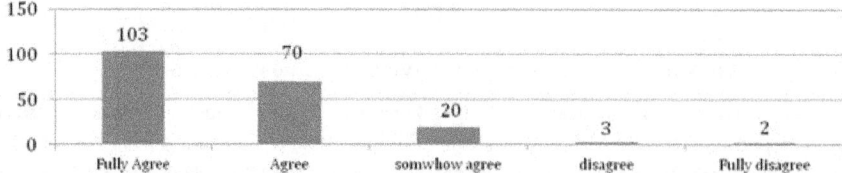

150
103
100   70
50   20
0   3   2
   Fully Agree   Agree   somwhow agree   disagree   Fully disagree

The survey also shows that nearly all of the respondents agree that the church should be a role model for ethnic unity in the society (Figure 5). This means that church members regard the church as the example and necessary means to positively influence the society at large. For Taiwan society, especially where there are large ethnic groups, ethnic stereotyping still exists and many injustices continue to take place in the legal and social systems. People may have to look to the church to see an example of ethnic unity and harmony similar to the Jerusalem church that enjoyed the favor of the citizens around them and the Antioch church where the believers' testimony won them the

Do you agree that the church should be a role model for promoting unity among ethnic groups in the society?

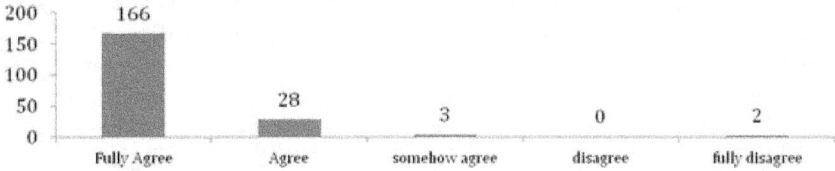

recognition as "Christians."

Figure 5

Percentage of Members Agreeing that Church Should Be a Role Model for Ethnic Unity

Over 170 people out of 199 are in favor and support of the church's new Hakka outreach plan (Figure 6). This means that we have this many people who are available for recruitment for various types of ministry among the Hakka people both at church and in the Meinong area. At present 30 Hakka speaking people are gathering weekly for prayer and fellowship. They are also seeking God's direction to lead them into the Meinong district, where many of their ancestors come from.

Figure 6

Do you want to support or take part in Wuchang Church's outreach to the Hakka people?

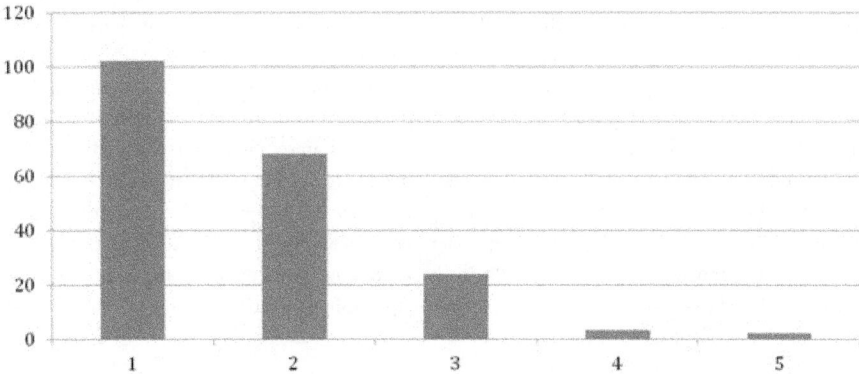

Support or Participation in Outreach to Hakka People

In-depth Interviews

The focus of the in-depth interviews of the four key stakeholders runs along the theme of having multiethnic ministry in the Wu Chang Church. The interviewer acquired the interviewees' verbal consent for verbal recording. The interviewees were all given the questions ahead of time for preparation. However, the interviews were conducted in a semi-structured format with open-ended questions. These questions serve as guide rather than specific questions to be answered. Many more related topics and applicable insights were raised and suggested during the process. Each of the interviews lasted about one hour. All four of the interviewees were interviewed separately to ensure maximum freedom for expression and to avoid disturbances. The transcriptions of the interviews are listed as appendices, 6-1 through 6-4. The following are the findings from these interviews.

Theme: Multiethnic Ministry

All interviewees are people who are aware of the programs and work being done for different ethnic groups within and outside the church, especially in the years since I joined this church. The most obvious is the addition of the English ministry, which now has been in operation for a number of years. The interviewees/stakeholders saw how the ministry adds to the multiethnic look of the church. They all expressed that the overall unity movement in Taiwan, in which the Wu Chang Church has been the key church in the south of Taiwan, gives the church members a clear sense of unity among diversity. However, these stakeholders, although not opposed to any multiethnic ministry in the church, all expressed that it is not the framework from which they operate. This means that multiethnic ministry to them remains an aspirational goal, a good thing to have yet still on the fringe of church operations. Pastor David said, "I don't see the multiethnic ministry becoming a focal point of this church at this juncture yet." Pastor David is in charge of this church's Hakka prayer fellowship and education department.

Each of the interviewees has had some form of contribution to the ethnic ministry of Wu Chang Church. They might not see the bigger picture of multiethnicity in the church or feel compelled by the need for multiethnic ministry in this church. However, they have inadvertently contributed to the advancement of this ministry. From their sharing, I received the impression that all of them have willing spirits to see the kingdom of God advance through this church, so for them any work that the Lord stirs up in this church is a work with which they would like to become involved. Pearl had personally arranged for eight classes of new residents to attend an orientation in conjunction with the Social Welfare Department of Kaohsiung City. She says she is open to restarting these classes or any other meaningful outreach and service to foreign spouses and foreign workers. Pastor Ruth's fellowship of career women has the most foreign spouses from Mainland China and Southeast Asian countries like Thailand and Vietnam. Pastor David shares that out of obedience to the senior pastor, he has been taking the lead in the Hakka prayer fellowship since July of 2012.

Multiethnic Ministry and the Wu Chang

Church

Like many churches in the south of Taiwan where the majority of the population speak Taiwanese, a variant of the Hokkien language of China, Wu Chang conducted her service in Taiwanese and later, after the church relocated to Ling-Chuang Street near the city's cultural center, the church began to have two language services, i.e. Taiwanese and Mandarin. The Taiwanese service is by and large attended by older members, who speak Taiwanese as their mother tongue, or transfer members from the Taiwanese-speaking Presbyterian churches in Taiwan. The mainlanders and second generation Taiwanese go to the Mandarin services. In October 2010, I was invited to join Wu Chang Church, where I earlier had attended seven years, before going to the United States for theological education, followed by a pastorate from 1996 to 2010 at Galilee South Community Church in Denver, Colorado. After moving the whole family back to our home country, because of my experience, expertise, and networking, I was given the task of expanding the church's missions programs, both domestic and foreign. The overall goal is to expand the church's outreach to the growing international community around her while preparing her membership for cross-cultural missions.

I conducted a preliminary study of multiethnic ministries in Taiwan and Kaohsiung and networked with various pastors and churches engaged in multiethnic ministries when I attended the Conservative Baptist Global conference held at Wu Chang in October 2010. After a visit to the Banner Church in Taichung, where there are outreaches to internationals in the church via English programs, I created an English ministry under the existing Wu Chang Church's organization. The most visible change to the Sunday service was the addition of a professional interpreting system (and booths), which allows simultaneous interpretation for two languages. With the addition of this hardware, the church commenced simultaneous interpretation for the second and third service from Mandarin to English. A team of interpreters was assembled and trained to provide such service. The Sunday sermon notes on projection are now bilingual. With the installation of this equipment and training for translation service, the church is now providing weekly English interpretation for international visitors and conferences with international guests. Many church members also use this service to improve their English. The goals for this English interpretation and bilingual presentation are both short-term, i.e., the simultaneous interpretation provided in the English language for English-speaking visitors, and long-term, to use such a weekly operation to train a group of interpreters for conferences and future foreign missionary service. These were all included in my proposal to the deacon board in order to gain approval to proceed for starting the English ministry.

The Beginning of the English/Mandarin Bilingual Service at Wu Chang

The Senior Pastor invited me to this church to help propel the church into cross-cultural ministries, both domestic and international. I proposed to the church deacon board the plan to launch an English Ministry in October of 2010, and they assigned the task of planning and implementing such a program to me.[54] After joining the Wu Chang Church staff, I set in motion a series of actions in preparation for the church to begin the English Ministry. The actions included conducting a survey of the church regarding the interest and need for adding an English ministry to the existing church

---

[54] Meeting Minutes of October, 2010 of the Wu Chang Church. See the Wu Chang Church Multiethnic Ministry Timeline created by the author listed as Appendix 2.

programs. A Question & Answer session was conducted to meet and interact with potentially interested people. There were a couple of events, such as a Thanksgiving dinner and Christmas English program. After a preliminary study and testing the temperature, a proposal to begin the English Ministry was submitted to the church deacon board in October of 2010. Based on the findings of the general membership and interest expressed by the same, the proposed English Ministry's vision was written as " to broaden the scope of outreach by the Wu Chang Church to reach both locals and internationals in three concentric circles, i.e. Kaohsiung, Taiwan, and abroad. The three concentric circles model was adopted from the Acts 1:8 concept of being witnesses for Christ from Jerusalem, Judea and Samaria, and to the ends of the earth.

The Goals of the English Ministry of the Wu Chang Church

Guided by the vision, the English Ministry of the Wu Chang Church set three specific goals. The first and the primary one was to prepare the Wu Chang Church members to be cross-cultural Kingdom workers who understand the call for world missions, especially the Back to Jerusalem Movement (BJM). A large number of church members studied overseas, mostly in English-speaking countries like the U.S. or the U.K.. Yet when thinking about missions, the church was primarily thinking about missionary work in China, or to overseas Chinese. There was little cross-cultural work being done by this church. Before the English Ministry was started the church had only sent four short-term missions teams to the Philippines. However, the majority of church members who were English-speaking had not had either the burden or the opportunity to serve cross-culturally. With the English Ministry, I set an initial goal to challenge and to train English-speaking church members to begin using English for church related work. This included English Bible study, attending the English/Chinese bilingual service, and being part of the service teams for Sunday services. Because of my interpreting background, I also organized the interpreting team. After giving a training session to become oriented to the skills of interpreting, I launched a simultaneous interpreting service for the third hour service on Sunday. This was part of an overall purpose to immerse the church members in a Chinese/English bilingual environment, where both worship songs and sermon outlines are presented bilingually. I intended to prepare the church membership to be familiar with reading and hearing English. All this was for the purpose of preparing cross-cultural workers, both short-term and long-term. The interpreters who were prepared through this ministry have provided interpreting services at several international Christian conferences in this city. A translation team was organized through the English Ministry. This team's primary duty is to help translate from Chinese to English teaching materials for Christian elementary schools in a Creative Access Nation (CAN), run by a BJM group, with whom Wu Chang Church has a long-term partnership. And for those who are more English savvy, they are encouraged to attend an English/Chinese bilingual service, for which I supervise planning and overseeing. The service was launched in March, 2011, and as of October, 2012, there was a steady attendance of 160 adults with two children's Sunday school classes. Through this ministry, already two cross-cultural short-term missions teams have been sent to South Asia (Nepal and India) and the Philippines.

The second goal of this English Ministry was to reach the international community in this city. I found out that because of the government policy of internationalization of higher education programs, universities in the city all have international students who are here either for language learning or to earn degrees. The first English gospel camp I organized was to reach the international students at a local university where there are students from Haiti, India, and Mainland China. Locally, this bilingual service has also attracted some international people. These are mostly international students and spouses of Taiwanese. The third stated goal was to use the English Ministry as a platform to attract seekers who are interested in learning English. A steady stream of visitors have come to this bilingual service and the English Bible study classes provided for students, young adults, and adults. Another group of people who have been attracted by this bilingual program, are the seekers who wish to have their children learn English through our ministries. Lately there were two age groups of bilingual children's classes on Sundays.

Missions Programs of the Wu Chang Church

Over two decades of the church, Wu Chang had been steadily engaged in local and foreign missions. Through prayer and participation, church members today actively engage themselves in various types of outreaches and short-term missions. Domestically, the church sends out teams in weekly outreaches to tribal areas of the greater Kaohsiung County. As of 2016 the church planted ten daughter churches in the greater Kaohsiung area, including one in the rural Meinong Hakka community, as well as one in Hengchun on the southern tip of Taiwan.

Internationally, the church supports three missionaries and their families. Since the early 90s the church has been steadily sending pastors and teams to various house church networks in China to help train local leaders. There are other missionary works, such as an orphanage and medical short-term missions, that are sent from this church every year. As for missions to non-Chinese countries, the church maintains a steady partnership with a missions organization called Action Missions (A Missions) founded by a Christian businessman, who is highly entrepreneurial and adventurous. The mission now trains young people from church networks for career work in Creative Access Nations.

Before I joined the church staff, Wu Chang's foreign missions was predominantly with and through A Missions. Since 2011, I have led several vision exploring teams to various parts of India. This was done through the network of relationships I had in the United States. Friends Missionary Prayer Band (FMPB) headquartered in Chennai, Tamilnadu, was the group we worked with in our visits to the Northeast, south, and north India. Another missions group with whom we work is a network of indigenous pastors in North India, where the least amount of Christian witness is present. With such partnerships, Wu Chang has officially entered into cross-cultural missions. And in March 2012, the first church-sponsored short-term missions team was sent to Nepal and then India to serve. This was significant for the church since the team was truly operating in a cross-cultural setting, reaching out to local Indians and training their house church leaders. As a result of these two-way visits, awareness of mission needs in India has been heightened. Of late, there have been exploratory visits to Indochina and southeast Asia.

The Unity Movement

According to a church report of Taiwan, conservatively, Christians make up 5.3% of the total population.[55] The number of Christians doubled in a decade. More importantly, in metro areas, the percentage is higher. In Taipei the percentage is 12% and in Kaohsiung 5.6%. This means that city people are more receptive to the gospel. What is more, the number of churches with more than a thousand members by 2012 increased from single digits to nearly 50. These churches serve as hubs for many church planting projects and partnerships. In Kaohsiung, the stirring for joint programs and fellowship has heightened since 2002. Wu Chang's Senior Pastor John Cheng, who serves as the chairman for the Kaohsiung Pastors Unity Prayer Fellowship (KPUPF), felt the call to band together with some like-minded pastors from different denominations to pray and fellowship in 2001. They vowed to stay together for weekly fellowship and prayer for the city's transformation. In 2012 the fellowship had a membership of over 100 pastors from more than 10 denominations. Of the 400 plus churches in Kaohsiung, KPUPF is the largest pastors' fellowship and most recognized. Under KPUPF there are eight other subgroups, each with its own particular focus and networking. Through KPUPF, there are joint events like the annual Global Day of Prayer in Kaohsiung and city-wide evangelistic events, including taking the lead in the city as part of the Chinese Homecoming Movement. The Chinese Homecoming Movement is relevant to this research because this is the most influential unity movement that is taking Chinese Christians both overseas and to Mainland China, especially connecting with the house church networks. The movement was started by an Egypt-born physician turned pastor and another Chinese pastor from Vancouver, Canada. The first time the two came to Taiwan was in 2001. Both came with the vision to unite the Chinese churches in Taiwan, Hong Kong, and the mainland based on their experience in Canada of bringing together the different Canadian churches. The two pastors sought out key leaders in Taiwan to share about the vision of unity.

Some of the key leaders in Taiwan responded favorably, including Pastor Nathaniel Zhou, the former senior pastor of the Bread of Life Church network, which is the fastest growing church planting denomination among overseas Chinese churches. Pastor John Cheng of Wu Chang Church also signed on to this call. With the two of them on board, the north and the south of Taiwan were mobilized to join this movement. By the time I joined the Wu Chang Church staff in October 2010, the movement had held a conference in Hong Kong with 5,000 people in attendance. During the conference, the keynote speaker led the Hong Kong church representatives in a reconciliation service with the mainlanders at the conference, addressing the past hurts and stereotypes that each side had toward one another. This movement continues to sweep over the overseas Chinese churches. In Taiwan, the movement brought reconciliation among various ethnic churches and denominations. In April 2012 Kaohsiung hosted Taiwan's first Chinese Homecoming gathering with 8,000 in attendance. This momentum joined the coming together of five house church networks in China and the Hong Kong churches. In June 2012, 12,000 people from China, Taiwan, and Hong Kong, along with people from 20 other nations, were present in Hong Kong to witness the emerging of the Chinese house church networks unifying as one. For the first time, the house church leaders took visible roles in an

---

[55] According to the a nation-wide survey conducted by Cheng Chi University in October 2011 which was officially released in January 2013, practicing Christians in Taiwan including Protestant and Catholic make up 5.3% of the total population. Interestingly, 18.3% of the population professed Christ as Lord. 國度復興報. <http://krtnews.com.tw/country/item/4545-2012年基督信仰與社會研究調查報告> 02.28.13.

international conference and spoke to the audience about their intention to rise up for world missions. The Taiwan Church, on the other hand, finds her calling to be key to unleash the Chinese Church for world missions. To find her place in this calling, Taiwan churches need to be united on the home front to move in the same direction.

I found that through such a movement, the unity in diversity among the ethnic groups in the church in Taiwan has brought the opportunity for the Church to influence Taiwan society to the forefront. Ethnic divides have deepened the political polarization of Taiwan. In recent years, the antagonism among the two leading political parties, i.e. the Kuomintang (KMT) and the Democratic Progressive Party (DPP), nearly split the country in half. As a result, the country has suffered economic stagnation, and populist politics dominates society. The situation was further complicated by the magnetic draw of China with its rising economic and regional influence. The KMT wants to walk closer with China while holding on to Taiwan's autonomy; whereas the DPP seeks a more meaningful distancing from China. In such a climate, the unity movement of the Church brings fresh air to Taiwan's society. Even though the Taiwan church has yet to see its impact on society as a whole, there is already a ray of hope at the end of the tunnel. In such a time as this, the multiethnic unity within a church can serve as a testimony to the society that Jesus and His cross truly can bring down the dividing walls of hostility, and the church can be the agent of peace to the society (Eph. 2:14).

The Plan and Action of MAT at Wu Chang Church

The above mentioned history of the Wu Chang Church pointed the way and inspired me to accept my calling to multiethnic ministry in this context after I was called back from the United States to serve at the church. After consulting with Enoch Wan of Western Seminary, I decided to employ the action research methodology to implement a gradual transformation of the Wu Chang Church to a multiethnic church. In light of the changing demographics of Kaohsiung, as well as other metropolitan areas in Taiwan, I felt it was timely and imperative to engage in gently shaping the Wu Chang Church to be multiethnic. I am also very much aware that without God's providence and the leadership of this church's agreement, this push for change would not have been possible. However, within two years of my involvement in this church, I witnessed how God orchestrated many key events and movements inside and outside the church, both domestic and international. It was with these signs of the faithful hand of God that I proceded with my work.

Multiethnic Action Team

Basing my research on the action research methodology, I understood that to bring the ministries in alignment with what God is doing in this church, as well as with the social demographic changes in Kaohsiung, the first step was to examine the various elements both inside and outside the church that I deemed relevant to the multiethnic development of this church. The preceding pages of information pertain to these important pieces of the puzzle that I employed to put together an emerging multiethnic ministry at the Wu Chang Church.

Following the principle of action research, I then proceeded to form a team of key players who are stakeholders and directly involved in ministries of this church. They were chosen for their roles as well as for their hearts for different aspects of the multiethnic ministry of Wu Chang Church. The team consisted of five people. The first one is the youth pastor, Samuel Lin. He was the secretary of this team. He was in charge of recording the meeting minutes and keeping track of the timeline of progress. Pastor Jasmine is the wife of Pastor Samuel. She was on this team because of her background in social work and interest in helping disadvantaged people. She is also trained in using statistical tools to help formulate surveys and analyze them. Pastor Jasmine has an extensive social work background and understands where to acquire resources for any particular ethnic group. The third member of the MAT was sister Dolly. Dolly is a Canadian Chinese who married a Taiwanese husband. At the formation of the team, she had lived in Taiwan for fifteen years. As of 2012, Dolly was in charge of the English ministry's small group ministry. Dolly spoke two languages (Cantonese and English) before coming to Taiwan. After she arrived she learned Mandarin, and now feels part of the society. She is an articulate person and serves as the Manager of Public Relations for Morrison Academy in Kaohsiung. Her role on this team was to provide an ethnic perspective as a foreign spouse who managed to blend into the dominant society. The fourth person of the MAT was Pearl, the secretary of the Community Care Association. She works full-time for this association that reaches out to the community around the church. One of her key functions is to reach out to and serve the marginalized in our community--the elderly, the jobless, foreign spouses, and caretakers/caregivers. She has working experience of dealing with city authorities in charge of social welfare. She was also the key person running the orientation classes for foreign spouses. I am the fifth person on this team. I was in charge of educating our people and implementing the plans set by the MAT.

Actions of the "The Wu Chang Multiethnic Action Team" (MAT)

The MAT first met on May 22, 2012 after I had gathered the necessary background information about the ethnic ministries in Taiwan and around our city, Kaohsiung. During the one and half years before the formation of the MAT, I took part in the entire ethnic ministry and missions programs of this church. After charting out the overall picture of ministries and work related to multiethnic ministry, I called the MAT to meet and brought forth the plan to consolidate the sporadic ethnic work and gradually give it a more concrete shape.

Wu Chang Multiethnic Action Team (MAT): An Action Research Plan

The following guidelines and steps in this action research was presented, discussed, and finalized in the MAT's first meeting on March 2, 2012.[56] For the purpose of this research, I first called a group of key players in the church to form a Multiethnic Action Team (MAT). As described, the MAT consists of key leaders of language groups and ministries who are directly involved with community outreach. This team came together to talk about the problem of this church regarding multiethnic development. Key issues related to this challenge were listed from an initial group conference through group discussion. Because the MAT was made up of relevant stakeholders, they were to come up with key issues to be investigated in this research. Although there were several questions I wished to

---

[56] Minutes of first Multiethnic Action Team Meeting of March 2, 2012. See Appendix 5.

investigate, it was important to limit the question to one that is meaningful and doable. From identifying the problem, I pointed to the future of a desired state of improvement for the team to see what we were aiming at and what that future will be like for the organization. For the team to have a focus, I proposed a question to the MAT for initial problem identification.:

Recognizing our community is becoming more and more ethnically diverse, in what practical ways can our church, and you as a stakeholder, act to transform our church into a multiethnic church?

Field Research and Participant Observation

Once the problem and related issues had been identified and a future picture was defined, the MAT began the next phase of investigation, which was data collection for the group to conduct a more detailed diagnosis. This involved field research and practicing participant observation. Field research consisted of conducting firsthand observation, recording or documenting what one observed in a particular setting. During this phase, I, along with other team members, drew upon multiple sources of information such as archival records, observations, survey, interviews, documents, and files. This included going to various language groups for observation and recording, conducting archival research of church minutes, documents, and relevant government records and academic reports. The tools for these activities included keeping a research journal, document collection, direct observations, participant observation recordings, surveys, archival records, interviews, and physical artifacts, etc. The MAT met and identified key informants to be recruited for interviews. A questionnaire made up of several questions was created. For this part of the study, the members of the MAT also provided participant observations as they were key players who personally observed and participated in several important milestones of this church in its multicultural ministries in the three concentric circles. Another source of information came from comparing my multiethnic endeavor in the United State at my former church, Galilee South Community Church (GSCC) in Denver, with the efforts and findings made here at the Wu Chang Church. This comparative study is presented in the latter part of this book.

In-depth Interviews

For this study I identified four key informants from the church leadership to be interviewed. Each was selected for their respective roles that have direct relationships with multiethnic ministry for Wu Chang Church. A set of questions was created.[57] The interviews followed a semi-structured interview format, which allowed the interviews to go along a predetermined theme, in this case, the multiethnic ministry and its development in Wu Chang Church. The questions were not limited to a predetermined set of questions. Among the four stakeholders, two were pastors, one a deacon, and another was the secretary of the Community Care Association. Pastor David is in charge of this church's education department and heads up the Hakka prayer fellowship, which meets every Wednesday night for prayer and Bible study in the Hakka language. Their prayer focus is on raising awareness to the gospel needs of the Hakka people. The church also planned a church planting work in the Meinong area where many of the Hakka members' parents are from. Many of them still have relatives or family houses there. Pastor David was selected because his role in education and Hakka

---

[57] See Appendix 3 In-Depth Interviews questions for Key Informants.

ministry will be instrumental in bringing the church's educational system into alignment with the multiethnic vision of this church, and, in a practical sense, implement one aspect of this church's multiethnic endeavor. Pastor Ruth is one of the two founding members of this church's missions department. She has a strong burden for missions and is an influential leader in career women's ministry, which had, in 2012, 35 cell groups in operation on a weekly basis. Many foreign spouses both from Mainland China and Southeast Asia are found in this ministry. She is another key person in trumpeting this church's missions in China. She has personally been involved in such ministry for over 20 years. I interviewed her to get her perspective on how this church's missions program may be restructured to accommodate outreach to foreign spouses and workers in and around this church. The deacon chosen for interview had been with this church for 30 years. Deacon Lai Jiantai had been on the deacon board for more than 18 years and served as chairperson of the church's deacon board for three terms. He is well informed about the history of this church and is directly involved in decision-making and the ministry of this church. I wanted to gain knowledge of his take on the concept of strategy for multiethnic ministry. The fourth person interviewed was sister Pearl of the Community Care Association, and she was one of the members of the Multiethnic Action Team. She was chosen for the interview for her past experiences in conducting the new residents' orientation program at this church, a joint program with the Social Welfare Department of the Kaohsiung City Government. She was designated to be the person in charge of future outreach to foreign spouses and foreign caretakers/caregivers.

Before any interview was conducted, I designed a semi-structured question form with 11 open-ended questions. All these questions were designed to draw out the maximum information from each of these interviewees about their experiences, knowledge, and possible actions for the church's present and future multiethnic ministry. The interviews were conducted with the verbal consent of the interviewees and were recorded for transcription and analysis.

Gathering, Organizing, and Analyzing Data and Materials

For the purpose of triangulation, three types of data have been gathered for this research. The first was the survey conducted on August 26, 2012 about the ethnic makeup of the church and neighborhoods around the church members. The survey reveals the level of agreement of the people surveyed with regard to their theology of the church on unity in diversity. Through the survey I obtained empirical data on the church membership's level of interest in becoming involved in ethnic ministries, especially to Hakka and to the New Residents. The second type of data was from participant observation by the members of the MAT. In the second gathering of the MAT, the team members each presented their perception of this church's present understanding and willingness to go multiethnic. The third type of data was from interviews of key informants (subgroup data) in the church. The data and materials gathered have been analyzed and arranged by categories for trends, themes, and patterns. Quantifiable data have been gathered without using statistics, rather, presented with graphs and charts. Other data have been organized in table form to provide comparisons. The purpose of the data analysis is to identify important elements or themes. These findings are reported in the next chapter.

Presenting Findings and Recommendations

The overall purpose of action research is to come up with an action plan that will help make a change to the *status quo*. The MAT worked together to implement this project and to validate results achieved in the process. This was performed in quarterly cycles from March, 2012 through November, 2012. During each cycle, the MAT members went through the five phases of inquiry together and guided the church in incremental steps. At the end of each quarter, MAT members met to review the progress, to record findings, and to identify the next problem area for change. Having laid out the guidelines and steps, the MAT then proceeded to implement the plans. It was determined that the MAT was to meet every three months to review and plot out the direction for the following three months until the project was completed.[58]

Survey

To find relevant information for this project, I designed a survey to study the church's ethnic composition, members' views on multiethnicity and the church, and their level of interest in getting involved in future multiethnic ministries of the church.[59] The survey was written with an introduction that highlights the key milestones the church has reached in previous years. The milestones include the unity journey that the church has been pioneering for the churches in Kaohsiung, the English Ministry of the church, and its stated purpose to help prepare Kingdom workers for the 21st century. The church also began a Hakka prayer fellowship in June, 2012 with about 30 Hakka-speaking members participating. The goal was to prepare workers for a church plant in the Hakka community in the Meinong (美濃) district of Greater Kaohsiung the following year.[60] The increasing number of new residents, which include both foreign spouses and migrant workers, also challenges the church to take more concrete steps for outreach to those living or working near the church. During the church's 2012 missions conference, a luncheon and testimonies were given for 40 foreign spouses to kick-start the church's outreach to these people. Actually the Wu Chang Church used to provide two years of foreign spouses' orientation classes in conjunction with the city government of Kaohsiung, but, due to government bureaucracy, the program was halted in 2010. With this survey I intended to reintroduce outreach programs to the new residents. The survey also spells out a disclaimer that explains the survey will be an anonymous survey and the information will be kept for the sole purpose of this study. As to survey of the ethnic groups the members belong to, due to sensitive ethnic identity issues, the survey only has three choices, Hakka, New Residents, and others.

I understand that if we use more selections such as Minnan or Mainlanders, some church members will not feel comfortable with it. The Minnan and Mainlanders in Taiwan's recent history have been the two major people groups that are at odds with each other. So in order to study the church membership's interest in getting involved in Hakka and New Residents ministries, the selection of "others" is chosen to lessen the possible ethnic tension within the church. This proved correct in that only one person surveyed reported discomfort in being asked about her Hakka

---

[58] Minutes of MAT meeting One on March 2, 2012. See Appendix 5.

[59] See Survey on Wu Chang Church's View and Interests in Hakka and New Residents Ministries. 武昌教會客家與新住民事工意向問卷表. Appendix 4.

[60] The Meinong district is the largest Hakka community in the south of Taiwan with a total of 42,374 residents as of June, 2012.

background. She answered in her remark column that she thinks there is no need to highlight the Hakka people, who she thinks have been well-integrated into mainstream society.

The survey was written and presented to the church's deacon board for review and approval before it was disseminated to the church membership on August 26, 2012. The survey was also posted on the website for church members to fill out on line. A total of 203 were filled out and collected, among them four were incomplete and were deemed invalid. All total valid survey forms were gathered and arranged in statistically meaningful ways using Excel format.[61] The survey was conducted in Chinese, and for this report and analysis the data is translated into English. The survey was divided into three main parts. First is basic personal information such as self-identified ethnic background, age, education, church membership, and residence location. Second is their contact with both Hakka and New Residents. Survey respondents were asked how many Hakka and New Residents they know who also live in their neighborhoods. The set of three questions is designed to find out about church members' knowledge about the theology of unity in diversity and their level of interest in getting involved in the church's outreach to the Hakka and the new resident groups.[62] Third is the value assessment part where questions that rate five levels of agreement to disagreement are presented to be checked for the level the surveyed individual agrees to. Questions such as do they agree with the biblical teaching that the church should be made up of the ethnic groups represented in their community.[63] Also there were questions that inquire about their intention to get involved in future outreaches to the Hakka people and the New Residents.

Post-Survey Follow-up Program

Following the survey, I initiated a follow-up program to honor the foreign caretakers/caregivers in this church. I designated the Sunday of September 30th, 2012, as the Foreign Caretakers/Caregivers Appreciation Sunday. I then gave a sermon from the Jerusalem church's oversight of the daily distribution of food to the Greek-speaking widows to point out the tendency to overlook the marginalized and disadvantaged people in society as well as in the church. During the month of September there was also a documentary recording the lives of four Filipino caretakers/caregivers who had worked in Taiwan for 9 to 12 years. The movie's name is "Money and Honey," two simple words that describe the dilemma foreign workers in Taiwan face when choosing to come to Taiwan, leaving their spouses and families (Honey) behind in the pursuit of money. The documentary, which covers a span of 13 years, was supervised by a Christian director and producer. I showed the movie trailer to the church to bring awareness to this overlooked people group now scattered and hidden in our streets and high-rise apartments. A total of 25 foreign workers of the church members' families were honored and received gifts and prayer during the service. Most of them were visibly moved to tears when prayed over. I then paired up with another church pastor to book a one-time slot at a local movie theater where the movie, "Money and Honey," would be shown. I invited the director to be present after the movie to interact with church members who would see the movie. All these were timely ways to prepare the church to move toward multiethnic ministries.

---

[61] The data are arranged in meaningful graphs to show relevancy in the findings and implications chapter.
[62] Survey, Appendix 4.
[63] Survey, Appendix 4.

Multiculturalism and Relational View of the Church

Multiculturalism is a buzz word in today's academia and a very loud word against the backdrop of today's world affairs. Multiculturalism, according to the Encyclopedia Britannica, is "the principle of not only tolerating but also respecting different religions and cultures and encouraging them to coexist harmoniously."[64] This is mainly a sociological and philosophical concept. However, politically it is a government policy of many countries in the world. Countries with a colonial past or that receive immigrants, such as Australia, European countries, Canada, and the United States, have all adopted various forms of multicultural policies. These countries adopt these policies because they see the vital importance of ethnic harmony and integration. After 9/11, the Western world has also seen that the conflicts of religions and cultures are potentially explosive, so a push for cultural diversity, respect, and learning about religions has become prominent in policy-making. How should Christian churches respond to this 21st century trend? We see many elements at play in this cultural scene: the fear of the clash of civilizations, the exchange of religious ideas through international migration, the rise of the internet age, growing global economic interdependence, etc. All of these are challenging governments, international organizations, academia, institutions, and businesses and yes, churches, to come up with a policy or strategy to cope with or even take advantage of this reality.

How should the Christian Church respond to this call for multiculturalism? Of course the church cannot completely sell herself out to this secular view of cultures which reduces the Christian faith to one of many equals. As Christians we believe that not all roads lead to Rome. We still preach Christ and Him crucified. We continue to worship the one true God, the Creator of the universe. We continue to believe that there is no other name but Jesus by which we must be saved. We continue to believe in the coming of Christ to judge the living and the dead. And there is a hell and heaven. However, does that mean we Christians cannot respect other cultures and accept one another in Christ? Do we continue to separate ourselves from people of other ethnicities, languages, social classes, or even genders? What is the Christian response to a multicultural society? I believe the answer lies in the Bible and the local church. There is a very clear revelation as well as examples of how God desires the church to respond in today's world. The church in Jerusalem began as a multicultural church: Hebrew-speaking Jews and Greek-speaking Jews. When the Greek-speaking widows' daily provisions were neglected, the apostles addressed the problem by appointing seven deacons from a Greek cultural and language background. We learn that because they managed the matter in a biblical way, the church continued to grow. The crisis became an opportunity. The church in Antioch is an even better example of a multicultural church. In fact, believers were first called Christians there because believers from diverse cultural backgrounds began to worship and fellowship together as a church! The leadership of the church was multicultural. Barnabas and Paul were themselves bi-cultural people. In short, the Bible gives us a clear blueprint and guidance for this question today. This is not a new phenomenon. In fact, multicultural church has been God's plan and picture from the beginning. "After these things I looked, and behold, a great multitude which no one could number, of all nations,

---

[64]"Multiculturalism," *Encyclopedia Britannica*.
<http://www.britannica.com/EBchecked/topic/941150/multiculturalism> 09.19.12.

tribes, peoples, and tongues, standing before the throne and before the Lamb, clothed with white robes, with palm branches in their hands ... ."[65]

With the design of church prescribed for us in the Bible (Gal. 3:28, Eph. 3:6), we need to develop a Christian version of multiculturalism and put it into practice. Some Christian writings have presented a Christian view of multiculturalism and called it Christian Multiculturalism. Peter Bolt, in his article "From Every Nation: A Christian Multiculturalism," explains the Australian government's approach to cultural diversity and reflects on how the church should respond to the idea of multiculturalism. He argues that though multiculturalism sounds plausible, one "could not expect a multitude of different cultures and world views simply to unite together."[66] There needs to be a unifying value or purpose. To the Australian government, that is to be an Australian or the common use of the English language.[67] For Americans, it may be the flag and what it symbolizes or the Constitution. There has to be something that all peoples of a country agree to embrace that is above their own cultural values and practices. But this is precisely the thing the secular view of multiculturalism seeks to eliminate. Deconstruction should be a means, not an end in itself. Otherwise, a multicultural society will eventually implode. For Christians, the common denominator is Jesus Christ. Under His lordship, we all need to strive to love one another, respect each culture, and to "'bend over backwards to reach them (all peoples). Notice that I become like them, in order to reach them for the gospel. This is 'assimilation.' I assimilate to their culture (as far as the gospel allows me) so that, by God's grace, they might be assimilated to the 'Christian culture.'"[68]

The second question then is how do we put the ideal of Christian Multiculturalism into practice? This question also leads to more questions. What will this kind of a church look like? How practical will this church model be? What are the challenges, and how can they be overcome? What would happen if we don't do this? And what would happen if we did? We will seek to answer these questions briefly.

In an urban, multicultural setting, a church cannot differentiate between missions and the mission of the church, because their neighbors may be from any one of the many less reached countries of the world. In this context, a church should have representation that resembles the makeup of the community; otherwise, she is not fulfilling her mandate. The theology of ecclesiology is a theology inclusive of diversity. This is the very nature of the church. I believe the HUP is derived from basically a sociological, rather than an ecclesiological understanding of the church. HUP makes what is descriptive, prescriptive. The result is division in the body of Christ that outweighs the benefits of growth attained by following the HUP. A multiethnic church model therefore, is a multicultural paradigm for church growth in a multicultural society.

"The Rabbit and the Elephant"

Tony and Felicity Dale co-authored the book, *The Rabbit and the Elephant.* The rabbit is an analogy of the house church which is believed to be able to multiply like crazy. The elephant on the

---

[65] Revelation 7:9.
[66] Peter Bolt, "From Every Nation: a Christian Multiculturalism," *The Briefing, An International Evangelical Monthly* # 37, 1989. <http://matthiasmedia.com.au/briefing/library/1410> 09. 20.12.
[67] Bolt, "From Every Nation ..."
[68] Bolt, "From Every Nation ..."

other hand is the symbol for a traditional church, large, clumsy, and reproducing very slowly. As the argument goes, the church needs to adopt the model of the house churches. It is a simple analogy. "Something that is large and complex is hard to reproduce. Something that is small and simple multiplies easily."[69] House churches are simple and flexible. They provide true fellowship in keeping with what the Bible teaches. And most importantly, they supposedly can "breed like rabbits."[70] The rise of the house church movement reveals a need to cultivate genuine relationships among church members. George Barna attributes the exodus of members from organized churches to the fact that in organized churches, programs replace genuine relationships. It is said that seven percent of Christians today meet in various forms of house churches. This represents a pendulum swing away from the institutional church of old, which focuses on programs, rituals, buildings, and organizational hierarchy. However, the pendulum could go too far, to where any form of organization is regarded as wasteful and evil.

An organic church still can function with a form that includes the gathering of believers in a greater body. The early church met in homes as well as at the temple. This is called the two-fold structure of the early church.[71] Moreover, the organization of a body of believers is clearly the stated purpose of the pastoral epistles. One may argue the pros and cons of mega-churches, yet a church building with its testimonial presence in a community is still valid no matter what its size. What's more, the world, which is divided still by racial, socio-economic, and gender differences, needs to see churches demonstrating biblical unity so that they can see Christ. They will know us by our love for one another, as the song says. So the solution to the disconnectedness of an organized church is not to do away with it and replace it with an amorphous blob of believers. It is a myth to think that a house church can function fully with the intended purposes of a church and not have its own challenges. In fact, any form is a form in itself.

The question of organization and structure will always be something with which to grapple. House-church movement proponents list all the "burdens" of an organized church, such as the focus on buildings, programs, staff salaries and benefits, etc. to make the point that the simple house church model is the answer.[72] That is understandable if one comes from a traditional institutional church where many ills of the organized church are the reality. Is doing away with organization the only answer to the problems? Some cite the tremendous growth of house churches in China since 1949 as an example for the explosive growth potential of house churches. However, meeting in houses is not the only reason why the church in China grew exponentially over the past 60 years. It was partly a result of persecution that forced the churches to scatter. So meeting in houses could be the result of persecution, not the reason for growth. One might say that the Christians in China stumbled upon the secret of church growth accidentally. Yet one should not overlook other examples of large organized churches in China as well as in other countries that are seeing people turning to Christ daily. This can be seen in some North American, Korean, and Singaporean churches.

---

[69] Tony and Felicity Dale and George Barna, "Introduction," *The Rabbit and the Elephant, Why Small Is the New Big for Today's Church*, (Carol Stream, IL: Tyndale House Publishers, 2009).

[70] Dale and Barna, "Introduction."

[71] George G. Hunter, III, *Church for the Unchurched*. (Nashville, TN: Abingdon Press, 1996), 83.

[72] "異軍突起的家教會," *神国*, 20.

Ethnic Diversity, House Churches, and Multi-congregations Under One Roof

House churches are not without their problems. In the book, *The Rabbit and the Elephant*, Tony and Felicity Dale include a chapter, "Unity in Diversity," which deals with ethnic diversity in the church. Here they are referring to the house churches they are promoting. However, there are no experiences or assessments as to how a simple house church can be diverse and inclusive. Actually the Dales were asking themselves the same question.[73] They do not provide any answer. The reason is simple: a house church does not have the capacity to include more than two cultures and languages. This is why house churches or cell groups can only be a ministry model for outreach and fellowship. Yet to be a church, there needs to be more than a simple structure. The biblical reference to the benefits of house churches and groups are all valid and applicable, yet in the Jerusalem church, for instance, members also worshipped in the temple together.[74] Most cell group churches see this need. Therefore, the Sunday celebration is emphasized. The answer should not be merely house churches, or churches with home groups.

The solution and biblical model of church should be a church of cell groups or a cluster of cell groups. It is a reflection of what the church has evolved into and shows in what ways both the traditional church model and the house church model have missed the biblical mandate to be one among many. It is also a plan to make the seemingly irreconcilable differences, i.e., ethnic and language barriers, work for the advancement of church growth rather than seeing them as hindrances to it. In the case of the Wu Chang Church, the way forward is to bring all language groups into her five congregations with three languages groups and the Hakka fellowship, all under one same vision and leadership structure, same mission and budget, connected through cell groups that are homogenous. The design is able to accommodate the heterogeneous nature of the church while at the same time providing the comfort of affinity and sense of belonging of a homogenous fellowship.

The Reclaimed Dimension: A Relational View of the Church

A relational view of theology is a reaction against a western theology that is primarily theoretical and highly function-oriented. However, the relationship among the Triune God should serve as the basis for all theology and its orientation. Relationship is the key in all four realms of primary interconnections: the Godhead relationship, God and angels relationship, God and human relationships, and human relationships. Church in this view should be highly relational. Enoch Wan of Western Seminary proposes such a view of theology to bring a personal dimension into the study of theology. Wan proposes that "relationship is foundational in the Christian faith and in practice. It is a prerequisite to systematic/practical theology and missiology."[75] Wan approaches this theology from an ontological standpoint and proposes an alternative to the critical realism which is relationally based. He calls it relational realism and defines it as "the systematic understanding that 'reality' is primarily based on the 'vertical relationship' between God and the created order and secondarily

---

[73] Dale and Barna, The Rabbit and Elephant, 159.
[74] There is some debate over what the early Christians were doing at the temple, which had its own Jewish worship, not only every day but several times a day. Some suggest that they were there to evangelize.
[75] Enoch Wan, "Relational Theology and Relational Missiology," *Occasional Bulletin*. Evangelical Missiological Society, Vol. 12 No. 1.

'horizontal relationship' within the created order."[76] Theology is not merely the study about Who God is but how He interacts with His creation. In such a view, a relational study of the church, especially of the multiethnicity of the church, is crucial in bringing out the real meaning of unity which Paul talks about in the epistles. In this light, we find a genuine application for such unity in the local church, and that this way of life, living out the unity among diversity, is foundational to church life. When this is the case, there is no room for segregation, no room for xenophobia, and no room for a total function-oriented church growth model.

The fall of Adam and Eve created the brokenness in relationships among the above categories. The cross is God's answer to the broken relationship between God and people, and among people. Paul calls this the gospel of reconciliation. In this view, reconciliation will serve as the fundamental dynamic within a local church. This relational theology finds its best place for application in today's multiethnic churches. This will truly be a testing ground of the ministry of reconciliation of saints and the taking down of the dividing walls of hostility (2 Cor. 5:18; Eph. 2:14). The findings of this research show that the majority of church members today still need to be educated, challenged, and shown how the dominant ethnic group in Taiwan, namely the Taiwanese, should relate to other ethnic groups among them. The finding also shows a positive sign that when a leader has the passion to trumpet such a multiethnic ministry, there is a certain percentage (20% in Wu Chang's case) that are ready to embrace the relational aspect of multiethnic ministry. This relational theology finds its application in Wu Chang through a public show of appreciation to the migrant workers among us. It is demonstrated through a public recognition that tribal people groups are the "first nations" on this island and worthy of our honor and respect. Their talents and cultures can become an integral part of the multiethnic life of the Wu Chang Church. Interethnic harmony can be demonstrated through this church to let society at large see that real respect and acceptance can take place in a multiethnic church where all peoples come together as a family. In a time when ethnic tensions still linger and mistreatment of disadvantaged people groups are seen daily, a relational-oriented multiethnic church will tell the world of the power of the cross and the power of God. Even as the church in Jerusalem lived out this relational theology in their context, so the Wu Chang Church can do in Kaohsiung.

Every day they continued to meet together in the temple courts. They broke bread in their homes and ate together with glad and sincere hearts, [47]praising God and enjoying the favor of all the people. And the Lord added to their number daily those who were being saved (Acts 2:46-47).

Summary

A church does not exist in a vacuum. It exists in a context. The first century churches existed in their individual contexts, where Greek and Jewish as well as other cultures co-existed. The church did not choose to separate, rather worked to include all. A church needs to reflect its context and surroundings where it is established. In today's globalized societies where most urban churches exist, ethnic diversity is a daily reality. This is not exclusively the case in North America, but increasingly so in most metropolises in the world. Peoples are on the move. They migrate, immigrate, and countries

---

[76] Enoch Wan, "The Paradigm of Relational Realism," *Occasional Bulletin*, Evangelical Missiological Society, Vol. 19 No. 2.

push and pull them to move across lands and countries. This is true even more so in today's flat world as Friedman calls it. A local church needs to be a mirror of its immediate surroundings and to reflect the ethnic and cultural make up of its context.

Of course if a church finds itself in a mono-cultural setting, there is no need to try to artificially make it ethnically diverse. In today's world, there are few major cities where we do not find other ethnic groups co-existing. The world has come to the local church. The question is: does the church have a theology that encourages or discourages inclusion of these ethnic groups? If a local church devotes itself to this form of church unity, foreign missions will cease to become a program or the work of a selected few. Missions will no longer be foreign but will become daily occurrences. The line between local church ministry and foreign missions will be blurred. Missions for a multiethnic church will eventually become a way of life. Relational theology aims at uniting all peoples before the throne of God for an ultimate oneness which will be realized in the new heaven and new earth. With such an ideal state of relational unity, church families on earth will be a daily dress rehearsal of the grand finale that will last for eternity. With such an expectation, the church cries "Amen. Come, Lord Jesus" (Rev. 22:20).

CHAPTER 5

DIASPORA MISSIONS OF THE WU CHANG CHURCH

Introduction

Having presente Traditional Missiology and Old Legacy at the Wu Chang Church d the findings through this action research, I here present thoughts on their missiological implications. To give all pertinent implications from the study and findings of this research, we would address the missiological implications against the backdrop of traditional paradigms of church growth and missions, and propose relational theology to supplement the highly functional orientation of traditional ecclesiology. Again, the development of this presentation is based on the research design and methodology of the dissertation, and addresses the research questions raised in the beginning chapter. In light of the emergence of global cities, which serve as the hubs of commerce, movements of peoples and information, traditional and mainstream churches are quickly losing relevancy to, and touch with, their contexts and the people groups therein. They are regarded by many non-Christians as relics and even harmful institutions that indoctrinate with an outdated ideology. We need to first examine why the church is regarded in this way. We can see some trends. We will list some generalized categories of today's churches, which may not be precise, yet will give a helpful overview of the contemporary Christian church landscape. Not all churches are the same. There are nominal churches, traditional churches that have become irrelevant, emerging churches that seek to be relevant to post-modern people, and other non-conventional churches like house churches and even web-churches. All of these churches should be seen against a multiethnic/multicultural backdrop of globalization of the 21st century.

Traditional Missiology and Old Legacy at the Wu Chang Church

Traditional churches see missions as sending and supporting missionarie Segregated Still s to faraway countries, learning strange languages, eating exotic foods, and wearing funny clothes. They may have a missionary budget and hold annual missions conferences, where furloughing missionaries tell countless quaint stories. Take the U.S. context for example: despite the fact that churches can find peoples in their communities from virtually all parts of the world, they continue to operate as if these people continue to live only in foreign lands and jungles. Missions, to churches like these, remains an item in the missions budget, a necessary expense and program to indicate that they are still missions-minded, yet missions has nearly nothing to do with their daily operations. Missions is a program, not a way of life.

Segregated Still

The cultural landscape of the United States, and other nations for that matter, has gone through major changes since Martin Luther King Jr. spoke the famous words in 1963: "The 11th hour on Sunday morning is the most segregated hour in America."[77] The 1964 Civil Rights Act laid the foundation for the right to vote, to education, and to the use of public facilities.[78] And in 2008, the United States elected its first president of African descent. However, these legal and cultural breakthroughs do not easily translate to integration in churches. How ironic, since unity in and through Jesus Christ is the center of the Christian message. For centuries, many Christian churches around the world have lost this message. Instead of championing this message through their preaching and lifestyle, the church has given this role to the secular world. Ninety-two percent of churches across America are still predominantly mono-cultural. Of course, there are hard-to-break walls of separation between ethnic/racial groups for obvious reasons, like long term racial stereotypes, prejudices, language and cultural differences. According to a study, The Multiracial Congregation Project, conducted by Rice University in 2000, only 8% of all churches in the U.S. are multi-racial, which is defined as no more than 80% of the congregants from one ethnic background.[79] However, today this segregation issue is no longer exclusively black vs. white; it has become multicolored. The same phenomenon can be observed in Taiwan. At release of the data, the number of New Residents and foreign migrants in Taiwan reached roughly one million as of January, 2013.[80] If these two groups of people are pooled together, they make up a population twice the size of all tribal peoples combined in Taiwan. As described in the introductory chapter, the Protestant churches in Taiwan are very slow or unaware of this development. The Chinese speaking churches in Taiwan do not have visible outreach to foreign workers. However, Taiwan churches are very much awakened

---

[77] https://www.youtube.com/watch?v=1q881g1L_d8, accessed 06 23, 2018.
[78] The 1964 Civil Rights Act to the Present, *The Columbia Electronic Encyclopedia* 6th ed. Copyright © 2007, Columbia University Press <http://www.infoplease.com/ce6/history/A0858852.html>0 9.19. 12.
[79] Amanda Greene, "Sunday Mornings Still Largely Remain Segregated," *Star News Online*. <http://www.starnewsonline.com/article/20081107/ARTICLES/811070255> 09.19.12.
[80] At release of the data, the total number of legally registered foreign workers was 483,921, and the number of foreign spouses was 446,143 as of February, 2011. Taiwan National Immigration Agency. <http://www.immigration.gov.tw/lp.asp?ctNode=29986&CtUnit=16677&BaseDSD=7&mp=2> 02.28.13.

to the call for global missions today. I believe now is an important time to introduce the idea of multiethnic ministries to Taiwan churches so that they do not only look to foreign countries for missions.

Old Habits Die Hard

The Church Growth School of the '70s at Fuller Seminary helped promote the Homogeneous Unit Principle (HUP), which was coined by Donald McGavran. The HUP has been the dominant principle for developing churches and conducting cross-cultural missions even until today. Many reviews and critiques of this school of thought have been written.[81] The most famous quote of Donald McGavran in his book, *Understanding Church Growth*, is, "People like to become Christians without crossing racial, linguistic, or class barriers."[82] This basic concept serves as the underlying rationale for targeting people groups and focusing on reaching these groups one-by-one. This may be a good idea related to evangelism, though to build a church using only this theory is undercutting the church at her very core of being, i.e., what makes a church, church. Paul, in Ephesians, tells us that the early church apostles of Jesus Christ were given the revelation of the mystery of Christ, which was hidden from previous generations and now is revealed. God's heart is for the church, the body of Christ, to be made up of all the peoples of the world, of all socio-economic levels, and of both men and women (Eph. 3:6, Gal. 3:28). When we look at what Paul has revealed to us about the nature of the church, God actually is gathering His children through Jesus Christ as one family and one new people by abolishing the dividing walls of ethnicity (languages and cultures), classes (caste, socio-economic hierarchy) and gender (male and female). Moreover, with globalization, world communities are becoming ethnically and culturally diverse, and the local churches are essentially unprepared to cope with this development, largely because there is not a theology of mission that prepares the church to deal with the issues of ethnic diversity and Christian multiculturalism in urban settings.[83] In a multiethnic society, the line between the mission of, and missions from, a church is becoming harder and harder to draw. I believe a re-examination of both the concept of, and correlation between, the church (Ecclesiology) and her mission (Missiology) is needed.

The Problem of a Paternalistic Approach to Missions

Up until the modern missionary movement of the 19th century, mission-sending countries in the West, have for the most part continued to operate with a top down, paternalistic approach, seeing themselves as the experts and the recipient cultures and people as the under-civilized. Many times, it has been thought that to evangelize is also to civilize. Of course there were examples of the contrary,

---

[81] Wilbert R. Shenk, editor, *Exploring Church Growth*. (Grand Rapids, MI: Eerdmans, 1983). This book is a compilation of church growth case studies from all continents and reviews of church growth from both methodological and theological angles. The most direct critique of McGavran's HUP comes from the paper by Rene C. Padilla. "The Unity of the Church and the Homogeneous Unit Principle," *International Bulletin of Missionary Research*. (1983), 6.

[82] Donald A. McGavran, *Understanding Church Growth*, 3rd Edition. (Grand Rapids, MI: Eerdmans Publishing Co., 1990), 163.

[83] By using Christian multiculturalism, the author tries to differentiate his idea from the secular definition of multiculturalism, which is based on a relativistic view of cultures and religions. The author assumes the supremacy of Christ above all cultures and that all cultures are equal before God and the Lordship of Jesus Christ. All cultures can be purified and enriched by biblical values and truths.

like the story of Hudson Taylor and his China Inland Mission. However, even a subtle ethnocentrism, cultural supremacy, and expert mindset may cause an unbalanced interaction between missionaries and the so-called "target group." As Lianne Roembeke says, "One would hope that the western missionaries draw their self-understanding as leader from a biblical one, as servant of the church, rather than from the western cultural practice of leadership."[84] Of course the problem is not with western missionaries only. There is an ever-present egocentrism in every person. Ethnocentrism, "the practice of viewing alien customs by applying the concepts and values of one's own culture"[85] is an inner issue everyone needs to deal with. William Smalley also points out that a "full cultural objectivity is impossible, but an awareness of the vagaries of our selective ethnocentrism is very helpful."[86] I believe a constant reflection and examination of self is necessary for people engaging in cross-cultural missions. This requires that we who are engaged in multicultural ministries need to learn to see the world from biblical, as well as anthropological perspectives, that we might be able to deduce "from traditions and institutions the worldview behind them, which raises our self-awareness of our own ethnocentrism and increases our willingness to correct it."[87]

Theoretical Framework of Diaspora Missiology

People have been on the move since biblical times, however, never in human history has there been a time of such dramatic frequency and complexity of people movements as we have today. In the 21st century, "approximately 3% of the global population lives in countries other than their places of birth because of urbanization, international migration, and displacement by war and famine."[88] Originally used to describe the dispersion of Jewish people, the term diaspora now is a commonly accepted term to describe the spreading of people groups outside of their nations of origin.[89] The word diaspora "has been increasingly used by anthropologists, literary theorists, and cultural critics to describe the mass migrations and displacements of the second half of the 20th century."[90] Braziel and Mannur say that the meanings and multiple referents to this term are still being theorized and debated.[91] Ybarrola, of Asbury Seminary quoting Vertovec, Dufoix, and Rynkievic, says that the concept of "diasporas" has been defined too broad and complex. He proposes that we see them rather "as dynamic and changing communities interacting in complex sociocultural contexts in the host society as well as back home."[92] Applying the study of missions to diasporas, diaspora missiology then,

---

[84] Lianne Roembke, *Building Credible Multicultural Teams*. (Pasadena CA: William Carey Library, 2000), 59.
[85] Robert B. Taylor, *Introduction to Cultural Anthropology*. (Boston, MA: Allyn and Bacon, 1973), 34.
[86] William A. Smalley, "Respect and Ethnocentrism," William A. Smalley, ed, *Readings in Missionary Anthropology II*. (Pasadena, CA: William Carey Library, 1978), 712.
[87] Smalley, 713.
[88] Enoch Wan. *Diaspora Missiology: Theory, Methodology, Practice*. (Portland OR: Institute of Diaspora Studies, 2011), 12.
[89] Luis Pantoja, Sairi Joy Tira, and Enoch Wan (Eds.), *Scattered: The Filipino Global Presence*. (Manila, Philippines: LifeChange Publishings Inc., 2004), 28.
[90] Wan, Diaspora Missiology, 18.
[91] Jana Evans Braziel & Anita Mannur. Eds., *Theorizing Diaspora: A Reader*. (Malden, MA: Blackwell Publishing Ltd., 2003), 3.
[92] Steven Ybarrola, "An Anthropological Approach to Diaspora Missiology," 17.
<http://www.ureachtoronto.com/content/anthropological-approach-diaspora-missiology> 12.22.12.

is "... a missiological framework for understanding and participating in God's redemptive mission" among diasporic groups.[93]

Diaspora missiology involves integration of "... history, sociology, anthropology, theology, political science, geography, intercultural communications, evangelism, and Christian discipleship."[94] As an anthropologist, Ybarrola proposes that diaspora missiology may serve as a bridge to bring together anthropology and missiology, two disciplines that have gaps and even animosity between them.[95] Applying diaspora missiology to a multiethnic setting, Wan proposes an important concept that diaspora missiology is "... non-spatial, deterritorialized, not homogenous but multi-cultural and multiethnic and multi-directional."[96] Tuvya Zaretsky, of Jews for Jesus and the Lausanne Consultation on Jewish Evangelism (LCJE), proposes the idea of glocalized evangelism as a paradigm for missions to reach diasporas in a community. "Diaspora missiology studies social groups that are identified by ethnicity, migration patterns, or pop culture. They are either outside of their place of origin or are in the midst of transition. Globalization presents the Church with an opportunity to study various peoples in a state of diaspora."[97] The resulting compilation of the presentations from the 2004 consultation in Seoul Korea, entitled *Scattered: The Global Filipino Presence*, is said to be the first book that seriously studied diaspora missiology.

The 2004 Lausanne Congress on World Evangelization (LCWE) for the first time included diaspora in its Lausanne Occasional Papers (LOP), placing the topic of diaspora missiology on the agenda for the global church. Wan gives this topic a methodology, and established an Institute for Diaspora Studies at Western Seminary in Portland, Oregon. In his latest anthology of writings on this topic titled, *Diaspora Missiology: Theory, Methodology, Practice*, Wan addresses this new missiological paradigm from three angles.[98] In the theory of Diaspora Missiology, Wan lays out the perimeter for this paradigm in terms of its phenomenon, the efforts to theorize it, and its biblical foundations such as the Jewish experience, from which the term acquired its name and concept. Wan also describes the relationship between God's divine providence and human relocation and migration. Diaspora missiology is a paradigm formulated to respond to the phenomenon of diaspora and the shifting of Christianity's center of gravity.[99]

New Demographic Reality of Taiwan

Before one enquires into the background of ethnic reality within a society, one needs to know that the term "ethnic" is not a clear-cut word. Despite people groups' strong ethnic identity,

---

[93] See "Seoul Declaration on Diaspora Missiology," 2009.
[94] Sadiri Joy Tira, *Filipino Kingdom Workers: An Ethnographic Study in Diaspora Missiology*. (Dissertation for D. Miss., Western Seminary, Portland, OR, 2008). 19.
[95] Ybarrola, "An Anthropological Approach ..." 2.
[96] Wan, *Diaspora Missiology*. 103.
[97] Tuvya Zaretsky, "Glocalization, Diaspora Missiology, and Friendship Evangelism," 2010,
<http://www.lausanneworldpulse.com/themedarticles.php/1280/05-2010?pg=all> 12.22.12.
[98] Wan, *Diaspora Missiology*, 17.
[99] Wan, *Diaspora Missiology*, 316.

sociologists have argued that ethnicity is a fluid and imaginative concept.[100] In fact, it is more of a social construct. "Ethnicity is a group feeling of unity and distinctiveness, a notion of their own essence and difference based on a sense of common history, usually combined with other characteristics such as sharing the same race, religion, language, or culture"[101] Ethnic identity, therefore, is an individual's self-awareness or designation by a social group. Through imitation and internalization of that group's behaviors, accepted norms, and value system, an individual finds a mental alignment with that social group.[102] Ethnic identities are not simply defined biologically. Having said this, ethnic identity is, nevertheless, a reality. It is strong in every society; and for this reason, ethnic relations are something a society cannot afford to overlook. Ethnic harmony is on the top of the agenda in countries like China.[103] The government wrote this as a national policy; it is seen in national and local propaganda and slogans. India, with its many languages and castes, promotes unity in diversity as its goal. Despite these efforts, ethnic tensions continue to grip the hearts and minds of the people of the world. Governments of immigration countries that have traditionally embraced multiculturalism as their ethos now are rethinking their policies because in a multiethnic society, the dominant group may feel threatened by the presence and practices of these ethnic groups, concerned that their original "way of life" may be threatened.[104] Immigration has been a force of influence in Taiwan. As an island territory, Taiwan has been receiving waves of immigrants from various countries and regions of mainland China over the last four centuries of its recorded history. The concept of ethnicity and identity was shaped over time through periods of colonization, the Chinese civil war, political measures, and globalization. The multicultural landscape of Taiwan can be drawn chronologically from its indigenous tribal cultures, to the early Han culture, colonial cultures, and modern and postmodern cultures.[105] The tribal peoples of Taiwan were the original inhabitants of the island. The actual number of tribes is hard to define, though it is generally agreed that there are 14 known and recognized tribes, each with distinctive language and culture. Anthropologically, Taiwan's indigenous peoples belong to the family of peoples called the Austronesians. Situated on the northern most tip of the entire Austronesian map, Taiwan's indigenous people are believed by some scholars to be the common ancestors of all the Austronesian peoples that are scattered across the Indian Ocean and the south pacific.[106] This history indicates the crucial role immigration has played in the shaping of Taiwan's history. Traditionally, Taiwanese residents are viewed along ethnic and

---

[100] Fu-chang Wan, *Ethnic Imagination in Contemporary Taiwan* (Chinese Edition) 王甫昌. *當代台灣社會的族群想像*. (Taipei, Taiwan: Socio Publishing Co., Ltd. 2003), 24.

[101] Lewis, D. Maybury, *Indigenous Peoples: Ethnic Groups and the State*. (Cultural Survival Studies in Ethnicity and Change. Boston, MA: Allyn and Bacon, 1997), 59.
[102] Yuan-Feng Kung, Understanding the Transformations and Deviations on the Ethnic Indentities: Children of Female Immigrants from Mainland China and Southeast Asia. (MA thesis, National University of Tainan, 2007), 11.
[103] In 2004, The Communist government of China officially put "Building A Harmonious Socialist Society" as its goal for national development. See *People's Daily News* article Chinese version.
<http://politics.people.com.cn/GB/1024/3187879.html> 01.09.12.
[104] From the 70s, many Western democracies embraced the policies of multiculturalism to accommodate ethnic diversity within their societies in place of earlier concepts of homogeneous statehood. But since the mid-1990s, due to fear of loosing one's way of life and a belief that multiculturalism has failed to benefit the intended minorities, there has been a cry to swing back to the discourse of integration. See Vertovec, Steven, *The Multiculturalism Backlash: European discourses, policies, and practices*. (London, UK: Routledge, 2010), 32.
[105] Yuan-Feng Kung, 1.
[106] Peter Bellwood, James J. Fox and Darrell Tryon, "The Austronesians, Historical and Comparative Perspectives." <http://epress.anu.edu.au/austronesians/austronesians/mobile_devices/ch05s02.html> 10.16.12.

language lines among four generalized ethnic groups: the native tribal peoples, the Hakka, the Minnan, and the Mainlanders. Similarly, churches in Taiwan have been organized along these major ethnic and language lines.

The Influx of Foreign Spouses

In the decades surrounding the turn of the century, Taiwanese society has witnessed the latest wave of immigration of spouses, mostly female (96%) from Mainland China and Southeast Asia. This was due to the warming up of cross-strait relations between Taiwan and Mainland China and the intermarriages between Taiwanese and Southeast Asians. As a result, the social matrix of the Taiwanese society witnessed an emergence of a new group called by the government, the Xin Chumin (New Residents) of Taiwan. Men in the less developed areas of Taiwan (i.e. farming or fishing villages), would acquire foreign wives through special agencies. The women who applied to these agencies to become "foreign brides" were subject to poverty in Mainland China and Southeast Asia, and through overseas marriages, sought a better life with greater provision for offspring. This occurred during the 1970's and is now common place. Nowadays, having a foreign spouse does not necessarily mean one of them is prone to poverty, nor were they necessarily introduced through an agency. It is often simply because of the globalization occurring in Taiwan, with more and more peoples coming from overseas. In 2003, out of every 3.1 married couples, 1 couple included a foreign spouse, and in 2002, of every 100 children that were born, 12 of them were given birth by a foreign mother.[107]

The Fifth Ethnic Group

This new group of residents is now generally seen as the fifth ethnic group.[108] Children from such a background are typically born to blue-collar families if they are in the cities, or scattered throughout rural and fishing communities on the island. Before these new immigrants acculturate in Taiwan society, their children begin to be born, creating a wave of "New Taiwanese" entering a school system that is totally unprepared for this new phenomenon. The dominant Han Chinese society has been slow to come to grips with this new development and has been caught by surprise. Only after the turn of the century (2000), have they begun to research social programs to address this new wave of immigration and its impact on Taiwan society.[109] Due to the lack of understanding and legal protection, the new immigrants have been treated with discrimination on the grounds of ethnicity, social status, and gender.[110] This causes them and their children to suffer from low self-esteem and to have difficulty fitting into the society and the school system, creating a new marginalized, second-class citizen group.

---

[107] Taiwan Panorama (光華雜誌), October, 2003, <http://www.taiwan-panorama.com/show_issue.php?id=2003109210088c.txt&table1=1&cur_page=1&distype=text> 02.28.13.
[108] This group of "new residents" on Taiwan is generally called the "fifth ethnic group of Taiwan" 陳定銘. "台灣非營利組織在新移民婦女照顧之研究," 非政府組織學刊. 第四期. June, 2008.
<http://203.72.2.115/Ejournal/3053000403.pdf> 12.26.11.
[109] Yuan-Feng Kung, 2.
[110] Yuan-Feng Kung, 2.

Introduction of Foreign Migrant Laborers

Adding to this social mosaic is the introduction of international migrant workers from Southeast Asian countries like Thailand, Indonesia, and the Philippines.[111] Although not a stranger to ethnic diversity, Taiwan, in the decades surrounding the turn of the century, has seen a rapid demographic change due to the influx of foreign immigrants and workers.[112] During the early 1980s, a period termed the "Taiwanese Economic Miracle" took place, which caused a sudden increase in demand for the labor work force. This resulted in an increase in local labor costs; in effect, it induced a trend where employers started to hire foreign workers during 1986, although at that time it was illegal. Despite the hesitation of the Taiwanese government, in October of 1989, a piece of legislation was passed to allow Taiwanese companies to employ foreign workers. However at that time, only certain industries were allowed to do so, particularly those which require manual labor.

As time has passed, the policy opened up to more and different fields, which eventually opened a window for a wide spectrum of ethnic diversity amongst the industries of Taiwan.[113] The Taiwan government also unbolted the door to international migrant workers to come fill certain specific types of work, mostly in two categories—domestic caretakers/caregivers for the disabled, and industrial workers. Migrant workers come on contracts of three to six years depending on country of origin and type of work obtained in Taiwan. The Thai workers, mostly male, are industrial workers; Indonesian maids constitute the largest percentage of domestic caretakers/caregivers.[114] As of October 2012, their number reached 440,000. The government has recently relaxed its control on the introduction of more foreign laborers. It is only logical to think that the number of foreign contract workers will increase in the coming years. However, the Employment and Services Law that governs this large and increasing number of foreign contract workers is by and large designed with a short-term fix mindset. It reflects that the government does not have a long-term goal for the need for foreign workers, which has resulted in a drastic lack of oversight of the working conditions and rights of these foreign workers. Many of these employees work nonstop and live in sub-standard conditions. However, a typical worker from Southeast Asia earns 6 to 10 times the wage they would make in their home countries. For female workers who get pregnant, sadly they can only choose to have an abortion or be deported due to the breach of their contract.[115] Despite such treatment, many still choose to come to Taiwan to work. On top of the poor working conditions and lack of basic protection and welfare,

---

[111] As of November, 2011, the total foreign workers in Taiwan amounted to 423,338 according to the Bureau of Employment and Vocational Training, the Executive Yuan of Republic of China.
<http://www.evta.gov.tw/content/list.asp?mfunc_id=14&func_id=57> 10.11.11.

[112] Taiwan began introducing large numbers of foreign workers since October 1989. By the end of January 2010, the number of these workers reached 350,000. About half are factory workers and half domestic helpers. See Chinese web page, 韋薇, "天主教會對移工的社會服務," 天主教社區發展季刊/第180期.
<http://sowf.moi.gov.tw/19/quarterly/data/130/14.pdf> 12.26.11.

[113] Hui-Lin Wu, Wang Su Wan, "The Trend in Foreign Workers, Economic Linkage and Policy in Taiwan," *Journal of Population Studies*. (Taipei, Taiwan: National Taiwan University, 2001).
<http://ejournal.press.ntu.edu.tw/index.php> 02.28.13.

[114] 韋薇, "天主教會對移工的社會服務," 天主教社區發展季刊. 第180期, 1.

[115] 夏曉娟, "全球化下的台灣移民／移工問題."

<http://cc.shu.edu.tw/~e62/NewSiteData/Teacher/Hsia/Hsia_file/移民工研究文獻評論.pdf>, 342. 10.17.12.

each contract worker is charged a large "agent commission fee" which may be as high as their first one and a half year's wages. This becomes the heaviest shackle on these workers.[116]

The Catholic Church's Mission to New Residents and Migrants in Taiwan

Established religions in Taiwan have responded in varying degrees to the new development. However, the Catholic Church has been most responsive to this growing number of people and their social, emotional, and spiritual needs.

The Catholic Church's Mission to New Residents and Migrants in Taiwan

The Catholic Church has a long history of social services to the marginalized in society. In 1891, Pope Leo XIII issued an edict, the *"Rerum Noverum,"* which spelled out the Catholic Church's official position on protecting the dignity and value of workers as well as defining the Church's view of proper employer and employee relationship.[117] In 1991, John Paul II issued the *"Centesimus Annus,"* which emphasizes the rights of workers to be free from intimidation and poor working conditions. It also tells of the need for humane working hours, as well as appropriate leave and recreation for workers. The Catholic Church also noticed the phenomenon of international migrant workers in the early 70s. Grounded on these official pronouncements, the Catholic Church in Taiwan has migrant worker services in all of her dioceses. Based on the size and kind of migrant workers in their jurisdiction, different dioceses have various degrees and sizes of services for migrant workers.[118] Most Catholic churches provide masses in native languages for Filipino, Vietnamese, and the Indonesian workers. For social services, some dioceses also have advocacy, vocational training, and sheltering services.[119] And it was this very mentality that the Catholic Church carried forward, so that they were the first and most active in terms of providing refuge and care for the local workers since the influx after 1989. Various active churches, including Catholic Church's Bethlehem Mission in Taiwan, help set up churches near the worker dorms, along with karaoke centers, local food shops, and even provide work place health and safety training, etc., all to improve the quality of life for the workers.[120]

---

[116] 韋薇, "天主教會對移工的社會服務," *天主教社區發展季刊*. 第180期, 4.

[117] 韋薇, "天主教會對移工的社會服務," *天主教社區發展季刊*. 第180期, 5.

[118] 韋薇, "天主教會對移工的社會服務," *天主教社區發展季刊*. 第180期, 8.

[119] 韋薇, "天主教會對移工的社會服務," *天主教社區發展季刊*. 第180期, 11.

[120] Bethlehem Missions in Taiwan Official Website. <http://bmi.estyle168.com/english.html.>12.28.11.

Protestant Churches' Work among the New Residents and Migrants

Protestant churches, however, have been the least responsive, although some churches and missions organizations have begun to see the needs, and have responded with their ministry strategies.[121] The Presbyterian Church and the Bread of Life Church, along with various Christian parachurch ministries such as Tree of Life International Care Association,[122] Jesus is Lord Church[123] (a Filipino mission), and the Industrial Evangelical Ministry,[124] have a strategy to provide care for the day-to-day needs of foreign workers and spouses, including day care centers for children, assignment of care groups for each foreign spouse family, and community services targeted towards foreign workers. Although they may not be on a large scale, the relationships between the church and the people are intimate and personal.

As these ethnic groups populate the island, one needs to ask the question how the churches in Taiwan have been doing with them. Is there a working model that will help churches where they are located to take advantage of the ethnic diversity among them? Being missions-minded, the Wu Chang Church should seek to actively reach out to these ethnic groups within her city.

Summary

If there is a phrase I would use to describe the multiple challenges and opportunities of the multiethnic reality of Taiwan society, I would choose the words "virgin land." Over the last ten years, the church in Taiwan has witnessed a growth both in number and in the awareness of cross-cultural missions. However, there is hardly any talk of missions focus on diasporas within her border. This is especially so for mega churches and major Protestant denominations. For most Taiwanese churches, missions is still by and large "out there." We like to talk about "Back to Jerusalem" and reaching the unreached people groups. Important as they are, the one million migrant workers and new residents are here and rubbing shoulders daily with us. The mission field has come to us. The diaspora missions of the Wu Chang Church represents only a case study for the Taiwan church's response to the multiethnic mosaic of Taiwan today. However, there is light at the end of the tunnel. As we speak, more and more meaningful outreaches to foreign workers among us are taking place. A two hundred member Filipino church in the Da Liao area of Kaohsiung has five daughter churches (in 2012) and gospel stations in seven townships. Kaohsiung Friends of Indonesians (KFI) has played a key role in bringing awareness to local churches to reach out and care for the many live-in caretakers/caregivers from Indonesia who tend their charges and relax in various parks in the city. A partnership between

---

[121] According to the Taiwan Expatriates Caring Committee, among the 990,000 foreign nationals residing on the island, there are only 2 Vietnamese churches, 7 Thai churches, 14 Indonesian churches, and 10 pastors for the Filipino community. See Taiwan Expatriates Caring Committee website. <http://tecc-resources.blogspot.com/2010/06/evangelical-immigrant-churches-of.html> 12.28.11.

[122] Tree of Life International Care Association Official Website. <http://www.wretch.cc/blog/treeoflife/21951418.> 10.20.12.

[123] Jesus is Lord Church in Taiwan Official Website. <http://jesusislordchurch-taiwan.blogspot.tw.> 10.20.12.

[124] Taiwan Industrial Evangelical Ministry. <http://tief.fhl.net/tief/intro_et.html.> 10.20.12.

Taiwan churches and Indonesian churches has resulted in cooperation on both sides serving each other's missional needs. The Wu Chang Church now provides temporary relief for their Indonesian caretakers/caregivers during Sunday services, so that people who care about them can serve and befriend them. As a result, several decisions have been made to follow Christ. In 2012, Wu Chang sent out their first couple to Indonesia to answer the call for reaching the Chinese diaspora there. As we continue to bring awareness to this need, we believe that almost all churches, large or small, rural or urban, can begin to find cross-cultural missional opportunities around them. When this becomes the reality, missions can truly become a way of life for all churches.

CHAPTER 6

MULTIETHNIC MINISTRY AND DIASPORA MISSIONS IN ACTION AT THE WU CHANG CHURCH

The Church's Attitude Toward New Residents and Migrant Workers

To find out about church leaders' overall attitude toward New Residents and migrant workers, I asked two pastors and one deacon. They were in agreement that the church has a strong sense of unity even for her size. They think that there is no apparent prejudice against non-Chinese in this church. This perception is also reflected in the surveys received where 166 out of 199 responded with full agreement to the ministry to Hakka and new residents, respectively. This I found to be somewhat unexpected because the general sentiment of the church members and leaders of my previous church, GSCC in the U.S., did not give such a positive response as I observed at Wu Chang. The constituencies of these two congregations are much different of course. In GSCC, the majority of the members were from Mainland China; the congregation of Wu Chang is mostly Taiwanese. I have personally observed that these two groups of ethnic Chinese, due to their past histories, education and political systems, have quite different attitudes toward foreigners. The recent disputes over the islands in the East China

Sea are a good example of how people in China and people in Taiwan react to the Japanese government's move to purchase the islands from private hands. Overall, the interviewees expressed that the church membership will be welcoming to these New Residents among them if the church leadership gives more information and encouragement through the pulpit and programs. I find this to be quite encouraging.

I also inquired about the possible adjustments to the church's vision statement, strategy, or organization. The two pastors and one deacon responded with the comments that in general they do not see an immediate change to the vision statement for it does not directly relate to or disassociate the church from multiethnic ministry. However, they see the value of "unity" as one of the church's core values. These leaders commented that the unity movement for the Wu Chang Church as a prominent church in the south of Taiwan will pave the way for practical ministry to the ethnic minorities among us. These are positive signs in the adjustment made to the 2013 church organizational chart, which has been revised to accommodate for "language services" under the worship department. This allows the potential for all language groups to have Sunday services should the number of that particular group reach a certain level. Of course, another way that a language service was added was the introduction of the English ministry after I joined Wu Chang in late 2010. Today the English ministry includes a Sunday Chinese/English bilingual service of 160 people, six cell groups and two dedicated worship teams. With this development, the organization of the Wu Chang Church adjusted to include an English cell group fellowship that is made up of the six cell groups. For the foreseeable future, the interviewees responded by saying that we can see the establishment of cell groups for Vietnamese spouses in the Career Women Fellowship of which pastor Ruth is in charge. Pearl, who represents the Community Care Association, commented that for 2013 one of the association's stated goals is outreach to the foreign spouses and caretakers/caregivers as part of their dedicated ministries to provide mercy ministry and care for the marginalized. There is also a plan to restart the New Residents orientation classes when the need arises. Overall the interviewees gave a positive note and approval to the plan to include multiethnic ministry to the Wu Chang Church. They feel that the timing is right and that God's hand seems to be guiding the church and the community toward this ministry.

On the Three Concentric Circle Model for Church Missions

To accommodate future outreaches, I presented to the interviewees the proposed three concentric circle model for church missions and explained to them the need to begin intercultural ministry from Jerusalem (the church in the city) and move outward. Pastor Ruth responded with agreement that this is a good way of seeing the church's missions. She gave an example of how she led a Mainland Chinese wife of a Taiwanese husband to Christ. After the wife became a Christian, she had a great burden to share the gospel with her families back in ZhieJiang province. Pastor Ruth, who has been traveling to China several times a year for 20 years, traveled with her back to the Zhoushan islands, the lady's hometown. Together they brought the gospel to her family there and enabled them to connect with local churches. I designed the three concentric circles previously with this model of networking through familial ties in mind. I added to this and said if we as a church have a ministry to reach out to Indonesian, Filipino, Vietnamese, or any other nationals for that matter, we will be able to develop a foreign missions model which is directly linked to our outreach to new residents in our city. All of these will be relational and natural. On this note, the deacon interviewee also responded by adding the notion of working through Christians in this church who are in the business of introducing foreign workers to Taiwan. He suggested that we can use them as our portals in these countries to introduce Christian workers into Taiwan who may come here to work and be witnesses to their fellow countrymen. These human resource agents may also help place workers, who become Christian converts, to enable connections with Christian churches in their home countries. The interviewees were visibly excited when talking about these possibilities.

In the formulation of multiethnic ministry at Wu Chang Church, I increasingly see that a three concentric circle model (Figure 7) of multiethnic ministry is best in describing the mission and missions of the Wu Chang Church both present and future. This is echoed by the missiological strategizing and researching proposed by Wan as "missions to the diaspora, missions through the diaspora, and missions by/beyond the diaspora."[125] The fact is, this strategy is applied to and adopted by local churches as a missions strategy. I find it well displays the biblical mandate of Jesus to "be My witnesses from Jerusalem, Judea and Samaria, and to the ends of the earth" (Acts 1:8). There have been various interpretations of what these geographical locations represent. Some view it from a cultural perspective, from reaching one's own kind to gradually going cross-cultural. Others look at it from a more geographical perspective. When we look at the ethnic composition of the Jerusalem church, it naturally fits the geographical perspective, because on the day of Pentecost, the people who made up the Jerusalem church were people from 16 other countries and the locals of Israel. The oversight for the daily distribution of food by the Hebrew-speaking people happened in the first century Jerusalem church. So it is safe to say that from the first church, the church body was already multiethnic in her makeup. Taking Acts 1:8 as a prescription for the mission of a church, I can describe the Wu Chang Church's cross-cultural missions in the following three concentric circles (Figure 7):

"Jerusalem": The immediate context of the Wu Chang Church's ministries is the community around her and the city of Kaohsiung. This is the scope from which Wu Chang draws her membership and where she reaches out primarily. All the people groups within her reach in the city will be her potential target for outreach. The multiethnic ministry of Wu Chang starts from Kaohsiung, her Jerusalem. This is also the local cross-cultural ministry that we have talked about. The world has come together in most of the world's metropolis or global cities in the age of globalization. The "greatest merger," as Bob Roberts Jr. calls it, is between everybody's everyday local and global experience. And it should not have taken a 9/11 event to bring this to light to all of us.[126] It is true for the North American context. It is also true for Taiwan.

"Judea and Samaria": this, according to my definition, is the circle that represents the island of Taiwan and her affiliated islands. The Wu Chang Church walks frequently and closely with major movements and denominations of Taiwan. Through their networking and partnership, Wu Chang can help reach out to churches, parachurch organizations, and the government to provide care and outreach to all ethnic groups on the island.

---

[125] Wan, *Diaspora Missiology*, 115.
[126] Bob Roberts Jr. *Glocalization: How Followers of Jesus Engage a Flat World*. (Grand Rapids, MI: Zondervan, 2007), 16.

"The ends of the world": For the Wu Chang Church's foreign missions, this means to take on the mandate of the Great Commission and strategically work with churches and missions to seek the completion of the Great Commission and take the Gospel back to Jerusalem.

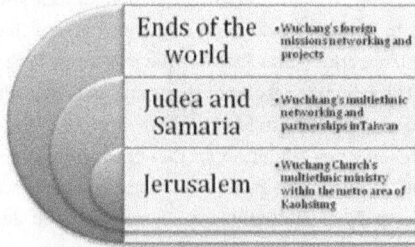

Ends of the world	• Wuchang's foreign missions networking and projects
Judea and Samaria	• Wuchang's multiethnic networking and partnerships in Taiwan
Jerusalem	• Wuchang Church's multiethnic ministry within the metro area of Kaohsiung

Figure 7

The Proposed Concentric Circle Model for Multiethnic Ministries

Kaohsiung: Wu Chang's Jerusalem

This is represented by the innermost circle of Wu Chang multiethnic ministry within the church and in the community around the church. This is the part where we actually make the church become more and more multiethnic. At 2012 there were a total of three language congregations, Mandarin, Minnan (Hokkien), and English, and a Hakka Fellowship. Within the Mandarin speaking congregation, there are three services with an average attendance of about 2,000. The Minnan congregation has 110 on average, and the English has an average attendance of 130. Besides Sunday services, the innermo

Plans for Outreach to Hakka and New Residents in Kaohsiung

After the summer's missions conference and Foreign Caretaker/Caregiver Appreciation Sunday, the MAT members met to talk about planning for the next year's program to target these two people groups. I took advantage of my leadership role in the English Ministry, the Community Care Association, and two other cell group fellowships, each with five cell groups, to plan for 2013's ministry goals and budget. My proposal was to conduct monthly visits to the elderly and their foreign caretakers/caregivers in their homes and in their neighborhood parks. Initially two parks had been chosen. Since Christmas of 2012, there has been outreach to 40 Filipino caretakers/caregivers from three nursing homes, and plans for continued outreach have been discussed. For foreign spouses, the plan is to reintroduce classes that will meet their practical needs such as Chinese and cooking classes. The goals are to reach out to them by showing God's love for them. Another plan is to partner with two other organizations that are doing outreach to foreign migrant workers and their spouses. One is called the Industrial Evangelical Fellowship, which is highly regarded as the best group to reach out to industrial workers in factories and major development projects. Another is the Presbyterian Church's Foreign Workers' Care Center, which provides temporary relief for foreign caretakers/caregivers, and outreach in the parks where they meet for social functions and daily walks with their disabled seniors. The plan to plant a church in the Hakka community of Meinong was still on the "to do" list in Wu Chang's church plant project in 2012. The proposed plan is to first plant a cell group in that community and then, through visitation and friendship building, the cell group will multiply into several. The goal also includes going into elementary schools and middle schools with our existing LIFE Education and Champion Education programs. Both of these are faith-based character-building programs that have blessed tens of thousands of grade school and middle school students. Another important part of the ministry within Wu Chang's Jerusalem is the Kaohsiung Pastors Unity Prayer Fellowship (KPUPF), which meets at the Wu Chang Church every Wednesday morning. Through this fellowship many city-wide events are planned and coordinated to maximize outreach to the various people groups and districts in our city. This fellowship has been involved in relief work among the tribal peoples in the mountain regions of Kaohsiung where a massive rock and mud slide resulting from rain brought in by a major typhoon in 2008 nearly wiped out several tribal communities, and remain disaster zones in 2012. Every time the city is hosting events, these tribal churches are invited and expenses paid for by the KPUPF. KPUPF is behind a city prayer ministry, the Kaohsiung House of Prayer, where there is 24/7 prayer and worship.

Judea and Samaria: Wu Chang Church's Networking Relationships with Christian Groups in Taiwan

The second circle of the Wu Chang Church's multiethnic ministry covers the entire island of Taiwan. Within the territory of Taiwan, the Wu Chang Church at present is involved in supporting a tribal ministry in Taidong (the southeastern part of Taiwan). The Bunon Cultural and Education Foundation was founded by Pastor Bai, a Bunon man who received the call to build a Bunon Cultural and Education Park. The Wu Chang Church hosts a youth camp at the park to help promote their agricultural goods in the city as ways of support to the tribal churches. Wu Chang's senior pastor feels a strong conviction to help and support the Bunon tribe in Taidong. This is a Taiwan-wide networking endeavor in the Unity Movement, which brings together several major denominations and mega churches in Taipei and Kaohsiung. Together they seek unity in diversity among the ethnic groups in Taiwan, first among the tribal people, then between the tribal and the Han Chinese. The reconciliation between the Hakka people and the Minnan people was accomplished in the 2012 Chinese Homecoming Gathering in the Kaohsiung Arena. Since the turn of the 21st century, ethnic reconciliation has basically been achieved within Christian churches. In terms of their place in the Christian church scene of Taiwan, the tribal peoples have begun to see themselves as the critical few that play an important role in leading the church of Taiwan in worship and missions networking with island nations of the Indian and Pacific Ocean.

The Ends of the Earth: Wu Chang's Foreign Missions

The Wu Chang Church's missions to countries outside of Taiwan, like many other Taiwan churches, began with training house church leaders in Mainland China. Over the decades surrounding the turn of the 21st century, since Wu Chang began her work in mainland China, there have been many networking relationships developed. The church has been sending out pastors and lay leaders in various types of ministries and has covered all four major regions of China. However, the church now has zoomed in her focus to China through close partnership with Action Missions, which provides missionary training for young people from the major networks in China. Besides working with A Missions, the church has also sent three missionary couples.

Diaspora Missiology and Multiethnic Church

Diaspora missiology is one of the key research foci for 21st century missions. Its importance is taken so seriously that it was included in the Lausanne Diaspora Educators Consultation of 2009.[127] Today is a time of rapid global movement of peoples and information. The world as we know it is shrinking by such movement of people and exchange of information. The peoples of the world are coming together in all the world cities, where missions organizations, denominations, mission strategists, and church planters target diaspora people groups and are forming homogeneous church groups and fellowships. Another movement today is to let the local churches take on this form of missions within one's city as a reflection of what a church really needs to be in a multiethnic context.

The presence of different cultures and people groups within one's neighborhood should serve as a wakeup call to theological institutions to realize that the world has come to them and cross-cultural missions is no longer merely about choosing or going to a certain geographical location to reach a certain people group. This diaspora missiology education was spelled out in the Seoul Declaration on Diaspora Missiology of November 14, 2009, as an arm of the Lausanne Movement.[128] There needs to be a rethinking of the correlation between local ministry and missions. Missions should be less of a geographical concept than a demographic one. Cross-cultural competency should not be exclusively for missions students, rather for all students in seminaries today. Missions education, on the other hand, should not be simply learning about countries and their peoples, about language learning and cultural adaptation, etc. There should be courses on missiological implications for local churches in today's multiethnic contexts, including reexamining the theology of the church and her mission, cultural anthropology and intercultural competency, multiethnic church organization and leadership.

On Multiethnic Ministry and Chinese Churches

Ethnic churches have been in existence for many years in Taiwan as well as in many western countries with immigrant communities. They exist for many obvious reasons. The first is for ethnic believers to worship and fellowship in their own mother tongue and to share a sense of belonging in a foreign land. This is particularly important for first generation immigrants whose language and cultural, economic competencies are still forming, which will enable them to become an integral part

---

[127] See Lausanne Consultations on Diaspora Missions. <http://www.lausanne.org/en/gatherings/event/12-consultations-on-diaspora-missions-the-roadmap-to-cape-town-for-people-on-the-move.html> 02.28.13.
[128] See Seoul Declaration on Diaspora Missiology. <http://www.lausanne.org/fr/documents/all/175-consultation-statements/1112-the-seoul-declaration-on-diaspora-missiology.html> 02.28.13.

of the mainstream society. The second is along the same vein though slightly different. Many ethnic communities use religious associations as a way to preserve their cultural heritages and ethnic identities. It is not uncommon to find Chinese schools and similar cultural programs being offered by Chinese churches. For outreach and church planting reasons, many denominations have missionary strategies to plant Bible study groups and ethnic churches in American cities. This is mainly for evangelism and discipleship.

These considerations are for obvious reasons as well: displaced people are most receptive to the Gospel when in transition.[129] This is also guided by the church growth paradigm of reaching people groups and forming churches along their ethnic and cultural lines. However, for ethnic churches to continue to grow, they not only need to meet the need of the first generation, be it international students or immigrants, but also the emerging second and third generations that grow up in American society, whose language, identity, and social groups are all moving away from that of their parents. The result of this, if the needs are not met, is that the second generation, born and raised in America, will not be able to find their footing in their parents' church once they grow up. This, of course, does not mean that they will automatically seek to join English-speaking Caucasian churches. There continues to be an ethnic identity that does not go away easily. However, a multiethnic church will make it a lot easier for them to blend in. The question is, if the exodus of the second generation from their parents' church is not addressed, will there be any real future for the ethnic churches? This is an unavoidable question and reality for all ethnic churches. Can there be another model for ethnic churches to consider, both based on Scripture and for the long-term health and growth of the church? I believe the biblical mandate and model for multiethnic development should be an important guide and example for ethnic churches in America.

The present day reality for ethnic Chinese churches in America is that the first generation works hard to reach out for evangelism and discipleship and develop church building projects. The second generation is treated mostly as a tag-along. Finding English-speaking, second generation ethnic youth pastors seems to be a never ending quest for ethnic Chinese churches. Even if some are successful in finding an English pastor for their second generation, they rarely grow beyond the third generation. The obvious question is why is it that second generation children go to school with other ethnic groups, work alongside people from different cultures and socialize with the same, yet when they come to church they only worship with their own ethnicity? Is the multicultural society at large more progressive in this integration than the church? What does the Bible say about that? I believe the biblical mandate says the opposite. In Christ, all the barriers have been broken down and removed. It is important that the church today live out this mandate. Of course we cannot be too naïve and conduct business with our head in the clouds. We cannot be overly harsh and ignorant of the reality that people of the same skin color and language will stay together. This is not necessarily unbiblical or ethnocentric, it is human nature, especially in a multiethnic environment like the U.S. and other industrialized countries: they need to stay together to find a sense of solidarity and belonging.

For GSCC, which grew out of an Anglo hosting church, its journey toward multiethnicity was slow. Their journey can showcase some of the achievements. They have engraved the multiethnic vision and philosophy of ministry in the church constitution: the church leadership has been organized to

---

129 Enoch Wan, "Mission among the Chinese Diaspora - A case study of migration & mission," *Missiology*. <http://www.missiology.org/missionchina/ChineseDiaspora-Missiology.pdf > 01.10.11.

represent the present and future congregations. GSCC has language-specific cell groups that serve as the receptacles for these English and Chinese congregations. They are the hosting church for a Tamil-speaking congregation, which in 2012 had not yet decided whether it would remain part of GSCC or eventually branch out to be on its own. Strides have been made in networking with like-minded churches and organizations, making GSCC known in the Denver Area as a Chinese church with a multiethnic passion. They have plowed slowly through ethnic and cultural ground, meeting barriers of ethnocentrism, miscommunication, prejudices, language differences, culture shock, leadership changes, organizational restructuring, etc. The Lord has prompted the church down a path less taken. My hope was that they would be one of the pioneering churches in this journey of faith and obedience.

I believe the multiethnic church development is not exclusively for Chinese churches in North America to consider. One key I found in this journey of guiding GSCC's slow transformation from a Chinese church to a multiethnic church was that this effort was spearheaded by an ethnic pastor (myself) in a North American context. The challenge was much more difficult in Denver than in a place like Singapore, where the Chinese make up a 70 percent majority, and where multiculturalism is already the policy of the land.[130] The elephant in the room is obvious. The majority of the congregation will not easily nor quickly buy into this multiethnic concept. In this progression toward multiethnicity, I was in an uphill battle against all the barriers mentioned earlier, with opposition on all fronts. Ethnic Chinese in diaspora do not see the need to move beyond themselves, and other ethnic groups do not see why they need to be part of this "Chinese church."

With this conviction in mind, I made a move to Taiwan in 2010, where Chinese are the majority and where diaspora groups are settling down in its main cities like Kaohsiung where I am currently ministering. The challenge for me now is to take my research and findings, and apply them in this land where the society is increasingly multiethnic, and where the same barriers to diversity and unity remain—ethnocentrism, indifference, racial prejudices, misunderstanding, and a long-standing church growth model for church development and missions. However, if this is what Jesus did on the cross, and what God has ordained for His Church to be and become in the new heaven and new earth, I am willing to keep doing the dress rehearsals in anticipation of that glorious day before the throne of God and the Lamb.

On Christian Multiculturalism, Intercultural Paradigm of Missions

The human bias in approaching cultures is that we tend to view other cultures through our own cultural lens and thus unknowingly confuse our theoretical models (relative) with the biblical data (infallible). The interpretation, therefore, is also biased. Even though we can hardly be completely objective and clear cut in our approach to cultures, an informed practitioner of intercultural ministry will be able to maintain at least an open mind, understanding and interest of other cultures, and a willingness to acknowledge a bias when confronted with the reality of conflicts. Dr. Martin Luther King's dream of racial equality is continuing to be realized.

---

[130] multiculturalism is already the policy of the land

A Christian multiculturalism that serves as the sociological foundation for diaspora missiology is timely in that the demographic of most urban areas in and around the world are becoming more ethnically diverse by the day. Today the majority of Christians are non-white and live in Africa, Asia, and Latin American. The same groups of people are in the U.S., and in our communities. Reality is, according to Soon-chao Rah of North Park Seminary in Chicago, mainstream churches are on the decline, and multiethnic churches are growing and leading the way into a more ethnically diverse future.[131] Christian churches should not let the secular world take the concept of diversity captive and watch it be twisted and redefined. Christian multiculturalism celebrates and embraces diversity as God intended it, not as the world desires. Embracing diversity "emerges not from relativism, but from a deeply held and aptly humble monotheism."[132] The rise of non-white, non-Western theologians and teachers is pushing the existing envelope of the theology of Christian Missions. Dr. Alan Lai of Mount Olive Lutheran Church in Vancouver, BC challenges the status quo of the dominant theologies and epistemology which has been "integrated to the internal colonial domination suffered by indigenous and nonwhite people."[133]

Multiculturalism should not be the monopoly of the secular and political worlds. The world has always been multicultural as God has always been the multicultural God. The church must take God's multicultural world seriously.[134] Speaking from a non-Western perspective, Lai puts it critically when he says that since colonial days a "westernized expression of Christianity was preached as the only expression of truth to the rest of the world," imposing its "universal system on all humanity, universalizing Euro-centric specific theological traditions," a Christianity "deeply infected with supersessionism, anti-Judaism, racial segregation, male chauvinism, gender inequality, and exclusivity."[135] Indeed, it is fair to say that even today, the systems of theologizing, education, pedagogies, ministry models, and philosophies are still by and large Westernized, which is highly linear, logical, structural, functional, and result-oriented. As the face of the Christian church changes and becomes more and more multicultural, demographically more diverse, and culturally pluralistic, Christian churches in cities must come up with a theology and ministry model that should not simply respond to the multicultural realities rather, it should take the lead in promoting a Christian Multiculturalism that will guide the churches' operations and development while engaging the larger multicultural context with the will, message, and power to transform society.

On an Intercultural Paradigm of Missions

Christian communication under the Westernized model, with scholars like Hesselgrave, teaches a cross-cultural model of communication. In his classic books on missions, *Communicating Cross-Culturally* and *Planting Churches Cross-Culturally*, he operated in a cross-cultural paradigm that basically fixed on this assumption about missions: missionaries engaging in "cross"-cultural missions are the experts who have learned about the Bible and the target language and they are there to coach

---

[131] Chris Meehan, "U.S. Multiculturalism is a Done Deal," CRC Communications, Laura Postthums, CRHM Communications. <http://www.crcna.org/news.cfm?newsid=1742> 03.30.10.
[132] Alan Lai, "Teaching With God's Multicultural World in Mind," 1.
<http://www.mtolivet.ca/articles/My%20Theology%20of%20Teaching%20Multiculturally.pdf> 02.17.13.
[133] Lai, 2.
[134] Lai, 3.
[135] Lai, 2.

the target people group about the Bible, about evangelism, discipleship, and church formation. Hesselgrave, quoting Eugene Nida's three culture-model of missionary communication, describes a cross-cultural communication paradigm that is basically one-directional. There is the missionary culture and there is a respondent culture. Therefore, in a cross-cultural model of communication, the missionary task is to "explain/communicate that (biblical) message in a way that is meaningful and persuasive to respondents in the context of their culture."[136] Where cross-cultural communication focuses on a Source Message and Respondent model, William B. Gudykunst in his book, *Cross-Cultural Communication and Intercultural Communication* (2003), describes an intercultural communication that focuses on communication "between" different national cultures or intergroup communication.[137] It is an in-group, or interactive model of communication that emphasizes reaching an agreement between or among the cultural groups involved in the communication. In a word, for me, a cross-cultural mission connotes a top down approach though not necessarily in practice, rather in mindset and attitude; an intercultural missions paradigm promotes equality between the cultures involved in the mission work. This does not suggest that such a model is based on total cultural relativism, which renders universal truth and righteousness invalid.[138] We will make the following assumptions as well: Firstly, an intercultural missions implies an equality between the two (or more) sides. This is borrowed from the multiculturalism we earlier talked about. Cultural relativism demands that there should be equality between the parties in missions. For this level of understanding, a study of anthropology provides invaluable insights for the development of an evangelical theology that is truly intercultural.[139] Secondly, an intercultural paradigm also means that there is a common goal for the parties in missions to cooperate in this process to achieve an understanding that is mutually beneficial. This is new knowledge that is achieved and arrived at by the partnership of the parties. Both or all parties in this partnership are learners as well as contributors. Thirdly, an intercultural paradigm also aims to uphold the supremacy of the word of God (biblical norms, non-negotiables)[140] and the person of Jesus in Christian missions. All cultures, whether that of the missionary or the recipient's, are both relative; therefore, they both are in submission to the authority of the Bible and Jesus Christ.

Summary

The day for intercultural cooperation is here and the need for multicultural teamwork and partnerships is imperative and urgent. An intercultural paradigm demands that there is a constant call to model after Christ's humility and servanthood in the process of communication. This can be called the incarnational form of communication. In this model, communication is over and above

---

[136] David Hesselgrave, *Communicating Christ Cross-Culturally: An Introduction to Missionary Communication*, 2nd Edition. (Grand Rapids, MI: Zondervan Publishing House, 1991), 109.

[137] William B. Gudykunst, Editor, *Cross-Cultural Communication and Intercultural Communication*. (Thousand Oaks, CA: Sage Publications, 2003), 163.

[138] Paul G. Hiebert, Culture and Cross-Cultural Differences: An Article of the Perspectives Exposure, edited by Meg Crossman. (YWAM, 2003), 94.

[139] Grunlan and Mayers, *Cultural Anthropology*, 252.

[140] The biblical norm or non-negotiables are different words used by scholars like Hiebert and Hesselgrave to describe the supra or metacultural truth of the revealed word of God and the gospel.

linguistics, customs, or cultural mores. It is about giving oneself to the other, which leads to my final assumption: The importance of an intercultural instead of cross-cultural paradigm lies in the ultimate goal of missions, which is oneness, a unified body of Christ. Intercultural missions in this light is highly relational, not simply functional. Enoch Wan's relational approach to theology and missions is a timely and crucial perspective in this age of multicultural societies. Intercultural missions' approach is not merely about persuasion and conversion, rather it seeks to create a new community of Jesus' followers.[141]

I have attempted to address the theme of Christian multiculturalism by critiquing the existing paradigm of Christian communication to provide a new way for Christians to confront secular multiculturalism. Christians need to be bold in proclaiming the inclusiveness of our faith and the heart of our God for the nations. The secular world of multiculturalism labels those committed to any faith with basic convictions as ideologues and bigots. As Christians demonstrate God's love and embrace all ethnic groups with their cultural diversity, the world will see that not only are they wrong about Christianity, they may also be blessed by the finished work of Jesus Christ and be reconciled with the Creator. In terms of Christian ministry in a multiethnic context, an intercultural paradigm of ministry and communication may enable Christians to see cultures in a new light, seek interaction, and an exchange of ideas and concepts between cultures in order to arrive at a new level of agreement. For Christian missions, we have arrived at a time of intercultural partnership and servant-hood. Missions today is about how Christian workers and organizations can come together to learn from each other and share each other's resources with a goal to expand the dominion of the Kingdom of God. This partnership can be in the form of outreach, church planting, social welfare, or community transformation.

When Christians across the ethnic spectrum come together in unity, this will be heaven on earth. This should be the ultimate goal of Christian missions. While we are still on earth where sin continues to tie people down as slaves, and barriers remain between ethnic groups, living out such unity may seem impossible. Yet it does not mean that we should not work towards it. Every Sunday more and more multiethnic churches are celebrating unity in Christ, living out the Mystery of Christ, and worshipping Christ as their Lord and Savior. This is simply the dress rehearsal before the real thing, when one day, with the devil defeated, people from all nations, tongues, and cultures will gather before the Lamb, worshipping as one. "You will summon nations you know not; and nations that do not know you will hasten to you, because the Holy One of Israel has endowed you with splendor" (Isa.55:5).

---

[141] DeYmaz, 21.

CHAPTER 7

CONCLUSION

In this book, we have provided readers a description of the practice and process of multiethnic ministry and diaspora mission in action at the Wu Chang Church of Kaohsiung, Taiwan. In recent years, Taiwan has not been exempted from the global trend of multiculturalism and diaspora phenomenon, and Wu Chang Church of Kaohsiung, Taiwan is a case in point.

To help readers understand the case of Wu Chang Church of Kaohsiung, historical background information was provided in Chapter 2, including a brief history of Conservative Baptist mission in Taiwan in general, and the history of Wu Chang Church in particular. Vision of the church that led to stages of growth was also reported in this chapter.

The development at Wu Chang Church in multiethnic ministry is neither accidental nor merely reactionary to the new reality of phenomenal shift towards multiethnic population; there is biblical basis and theological foundation for it, as delineated in Chapter 3.

The planning and process of multiethnic ministry at Wu Chang Church with a focus on the practice of "relational paradigm" within the context of a local congregation was presented in Chapter 4 and diaspora missions was presented in Chapter 5. Theoretical framework and practical implementation of diaspora missiology were reported in that same chapter, inclusive of Protestant and Catholic churches in Taiwan. It is within such context that we introduced diaspora missions at Wu Chang Church in Kaohsiung which has been reported in detail in case study format.

In Chapter six, we wove together multiple strands such as the "Three Concentric Circle Model for Church Missions," "Diaspora Missiology and Multiethnic Church," "Multiethnic Ministry and Chinese Churches" and "Christian Multiculturalism and Intercultural Paradigm of Missions."

In line with the global trend of multiculturalism and diaspora movement in Taiwan and elsewhere, this study on Wu Chang Church of Kaohsiung is a case study on multicultural ministry and diaspora missions.

The book's significance is summarized as follows:

- Firstly, it introduces the diaspora missiology paradigm to readers, a description of the practice of diaspora missions at the level of local congregation with missiological implications for Taiwan churches.
- Secondly, the survey of membership of Wu Chang Church and the narrative of plan and action in multiethnic ministry are informative and inspirational to other practitioners in parish ministry.
- Thirdly, the combination of multiethnic ministry and diaspora missions in action at Wu Chang Church is a unique case in Taiwan thus far yet can be easily duplicated elsewhere in this island and further. Chinese Christians globally are relatively less likely to engage in cross-cultural missions. This approach will be helpful to Chinese congregations to actively participate in the global Great Commission by reaching non-Chinese locally, i.e. "glocal" mission.

APPENDIX 1

圖一 —「出於聖經」與「合乎聖經真理」比較圖表

「出於聖經」("BIBLICAL")	「合乎聖經真理」("SCRIPTURAL")
聖經中記載/報導	聖經真理所要求
聖經中的先例： 非成肉身與默示的「道」所指定的	聖經中的原則： 成肉身與默示的「道」所指定的
特定的時、空	超越時、空
特定的文化背景或處境 (特殊性)	無特定的文化背景或處境 (普遍性)

圖二 — 溫氏治學 (綜合研究法) 五要
(聖、神、理、境、用) ("STARS")

CRITERIA	*	EXPLANATION
1. **S**cripturally sound	**S**	Not proof-text; but the "whole counsel of God" (Acts 20:26-27)
2. **T**heologically **S**upported	**T**	Not just pragmatism/expedience; but sound theology
3. **A**nalytically Coherent	**A**	Not to be self-contradictory; but to be coherent
4. **R**elevantly contextual	**R**	Not to be out of place; but fitting for the context
5. **S**trategically practical	**S**	Not only good in theory; but can be strategically put into practice

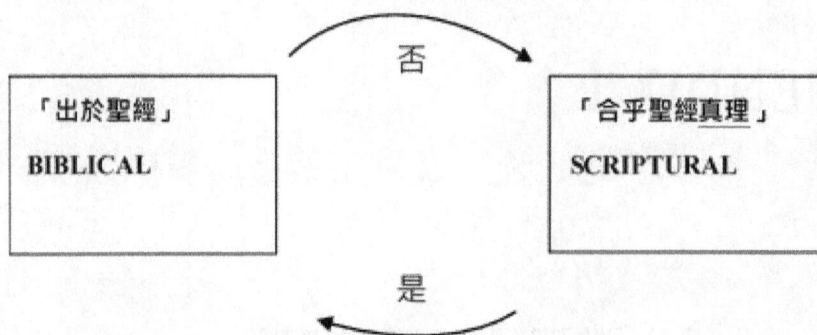

圖三 —「出於聖經」與「合乎聖經真理」表列方向

註:- 按傳統婚姻慣例，凡作丈夫的必是男士；但不是所有男士必是丈夫

同理：「合乎聖經真理」的必「出於聖經」；

但「出於聖經」不一定「「合乎聖經真理」

Center for Diaspora and Relational Research ("CDDR")

Western Seminary Press

Diaspora Missiology Series

D1   Italian Diaspora意大利散聚華人及散聚宣教 (C)

D2   Towards a Field Support Ministry Guidebook: An Integrative Study on Chinese Diaspora Kingdom Workers in a Creative Access Region (E)

D3   Engaging Chinese Diaspora in the Ministry of Bible Translation (E)

D4   Diaspora Missions to International Students (E)

D5   Missions Beyond the Diaspora: Local Cross-cultural Ministry of Chinese Congregations in the San Francisco Bay Area (E)

D6   Multiethnic Ministries and Diaspora Missions in Action: A Case Study of the Wu Chang Church of Kaosiung, Taiwan (E)

Relational Research Series

R1   Engaging the Secular World through Life-on-life Disciple-making in the British Context: Relational Paradigm in Action (E)

R2   A Theology of Spirit-Anointed Witness in Holistic Christian Mission Framed in the Relational Paradigm (E)

NOTE: (C) – publication in Chinese
(E) – publication in English

The titles listed above are a both in-print and e-book, available @ Amazon.com